EASY RUSSIAN PHRASE BOOK

Over 690 Basic Phrases For Everyday Use

DOVER PUBLICATIONS, INC.
NEW YORK

Copyright

Published in Canada by General Publishing Company, Ltd., 30 Lesmill Road, Don Mills, Toronto, Ontario.
Published in the United Kingdom by Constable and Company, Ltd., 3 The Lanchesters, 162–164 Fulham Palace Road, London W6 9ER.

Bibliographical Note

The material in this book was originally published by Dover in 1958 as part of a manual to accompany a recording entitled *Listen & Learn Russian*. The English outline was prepared by the editorial staff of Dover Publications, Inc. The Russian translation and transliteration were prepared by Helen Michailoff.

Library of Congress Cataloging-in-Publication Data

Easy Russian phrase book : over 690 basic phrases for everyday use.
p. cm.
"Originally published by Dover in 1958 as part of a manual to accompany a recording entitled Listen & learn Russian. The English outline was prepared by the editorial staff of Dover Publications, Inc. The Russian translation and transliteration were prepared by Helen Michailoff."—T.p. verso.
Includes index.
ISBN 0-486-28669-X (pbk.)
1. Russian language—Conversation and phrase books—English. I. Michailoff, Helen. Listen & learn Russian. II. Dover Publications, Inc.
PG2121.E17 1995
491.783'421—dc20 94-41981
CIP

Manufactured in the United States of America
Dover Publications, Inc., 31 East 2nd Street, Mineola, N.Y. 11501

CONTENTS

	PAGE
Introduction	v
Russian Pronunciation	vi
Scheme of Pronunciation	viii

	PAGE
Social Conversation	1
Personal Matters	3
Making Yourself Understood	5
General Expressions	6
Difficulties and Repairs	8
Baggage	9
Customs	9
Travel Directions	11
Tickets	14
Boat	15
Airplane	15
Train	16
Bus, Streetcar and Subway	17
Taxi	18
Automobile Travel	19
Hotel and Apartment	21
Conversation on the Telephone	25
At the Bar	28
At the Restaurant	28

	PAGE
Food List	31
Breakfast Foods	32
Entrées	33
Vegetables and Salads	34
Fruits	35
Beverages	35
Desserts	36
Conversation at the Post Office	37
Church	39
Sightseeing	39
Amusements	40
Sports	42
Bank and Money	43
Shopping	44
Clothing	46
Colors	48
Stores	48
Bookstore and Stationer's	49
Cigar Store	51
Camera Store	51
Pharmacy	52
Laundry and Dry Cleaning	52
Barber Shop and Beauty Salon	53
Health and Illness	54
Dentist	56
Time	56
Days of the Week	58
Seasons and Weather	58
Numbers	59
Index	61

INTRODUCTION

This book is designed to teach you the basic words, phrases and sentences that you will need for simple everyday communication in Russia. It does not attempt to teach you the grammatical structure of Russian, but instead helps you to express your needs and handle problems encountered while traveling.

The value of the book rests as much on what is omitted as on what is included. An effort has been made to include only those phrases pertinent to the needs of the traveler. You will find the phrase "May I have some small change" (a frequent need in travel), but do not expect to find a sentence like "This is the pen of my aunt." Furthermore, since the material presented here is not cumulative, as it is in conventional foreign-language courses, you need not start at the beginning. Study whichever phrases will be the most useful to you.

The focus of instruction is on what *you* will say. However, the section entitled "Making Yourself Understood," which contains such vital phrases as "Please speak more slowly" and "Repeat it, please," will aid you in understanding others.

This book is complete in itself and is meant to be used for reference and study. Read it at odd moments and try to learn ten or fifteen phrases a day. Also, be sure to take the manual with you when you go abroad. All that you have learned will be available for reference and review.

The book is designed to help you form additional Russian sentences from the sentences it provides. You can do this by substituting a new word for a given word in a familiar sentence. In sentences where this is possible, the candidate for substitution appears in brackets, and is sometimes followed by possible alternatives. For example,

I am [a student]
—a teacher
—a businessman

provides three sentences: "I am a student," "I am a teacher" and "I am a businessman."

Another especially helpful feature of the manual is the extensive topic and word index beginning on page 61. Notice that each entry in the book is numbered and that the index refers to these numbers. This enables you to locate information you need quickly, without having to search the entire page.

RUSSIAN PRONUNCIATION

The manual uses a phonetic transcription as an aid to correct pronunciation. (See "Scheme of Pronunciation," below.) It usually appears below the Russian line in the text.

Vowels

Hard and Soft Vowels

Russian vowels are classified as "hard" and "soft":

Hard	Soft
у oo	ю yoo
о aw	ё yaw
а ah	я yah
э eh	е yeh
ы ih	и ee

A soft vowel may change the pronunciation of the preceding consonant. (See "Palatalization," below.)

Stress and Reduction

Like English vowels, Russian vowels have their full value only in stressed syllables. In unstressed syllables they are reduced, becoming shorter and undergoing other changes in quality. The three vowels below are the most variable with respect to stress:

о In a stressed syllable, *aw* as in l*aw*, but cut short.
In the syllable immediately preceding the stressed syllable, *ah* as in f*a*ther, but cut short.
Everywhere else, *uh* as in th*e* boy.

a In a stressed syllable or the one immediately before it, *ah* as in f*a*ther, but cut short.
Everywhere else, somewhat like *uh,* as in th*e* boy.

e In a stressed syllable, *yeh* as in *ye*t.
Everywhere else, rather like the *ee* in f*ee*, but cut short.

The soft vowel я (yah) also reduces to *uh* in unstressed syllables. The vowels у (oo), и (ee) and ы (ih) tend to lose less of their character in unstressed syllables, although they do become somewhat shorter. The soft vowel ё (yaw) occurs only in stressed syllables and consequently always retains its full value.

Diphthongs

The letter й does not occur alone, but always follows another vowel with which it forms a diphthong. Be sure to pronounce each component of the diphthong separately; do not slur them together as we do with English diphthongs. The table below lists the principal Russian diphthongs and their transcription:

Letter	Transcription	Notes
ай	ah‿y̆	as in l*ie*
ей	yey̆	as in *Y*ale
ой	oy̆	as in b*oy*
уй	oo‿y̆	as in ph*ooey*, pronounced as one syllable
ий	ee‿y̆	as in *see yet*
ый	ih‿y̆	No English equivalent. Similar to *y* in ver*y*.

Consonants

Palatalization

A consonant is palatalized when it is followed by a soft vowel (see above). Palatalized consonants (indicated by a following *y* or ʸ in our transcription) are produced with the body of the tongue touching the hard palate. For example, palatalized *d* sounds like the *dy* of d*id y*ou (pronounced as a single consonant); palatalized *t* sounds like the *ty* of hi*t y*ou (pronounced as a single consonant); palatalized *n* sounds like the *ny* of ca*ny*on (pronounced as a single consonant).

The consonants ш (sh), щ (shch), ц (ts), ч (ch) and ж (zh) are already palatal, and therefore do not change when followed by a soft vowel. A soft vowel following any of these five consonants is pronounced like its hard counterpart.

Voiceless Consonants

In Russian, consonants are voiceless (pronounced without vibrating the vocal cords) at the end of a word or syllable, or when they are followed by a voiceless consonant. Thus:

b (б)	is pronounced	p
d (д)	,,	t
g (г)	,,	k
z (з)	,,	s
zh (ж)	,,	sh
v (в)	,,	f

SCHEME OF PRONUNCIATION

Letters		Transcription	Notes
А	а	ah	as in f*a*ther, but cut short.
Б	б	b OR p	as in *b*ed. *p* as in s*p*eak at the end of a word or syllable.
В	в	v OR f	as in *v*at. *f* as in *f*eel at the end of a word or syllable.
Г	г	g OR k	as in *g*o. *k* as in s*k*in at the end of a word or syllable. Occasionally pronounced *v* as in *v*ine.
Д	д	d OR t	as in *d*ay. *t* as in s*t*ay at the end of a word or syllable.
Е	е	ye OR yeh	as in *ye*t.
Ё	ё	yaw	as in *yaw*n.
Ж	ж	zh OR sh	like the *s* in mea*s*ure. *sh* as in *sh*all at the end of a word or syllable.
З	з	z OR s	as in *z*eal. *s* as in *s*it at the end of a word or syllable.
И	и	ee	as in m*ee*t, but cut short.
	й	y	occurs only in diphthongs. See section on diphthongs, above.

Letters		Transcription	Notes
К	к	k	as in s*k*y.
Л	л	l	as in *l*et.
М	м	m	as in *m*ap.
Н	н	n	as in *n*o.
О	о	aw, ah OR uh	in stressed syllables, *aw* as in l*aw*, but cut short; in syllables immediately preceding stress, *ah* as in f*a*ther, but cut short; elsewhere, *uh* as in th*e*.
П	п	p	as in s*p*eak.
Р	р	r	rolled with the tip of the tongue as in Italian or Spanish.
С	с	s	as in *s*et.
Т	т	t	as in s*t*ay.
У	у	oo	as in f*oo*d, but cut short.
Ф	ф	f	as in *f*eel.
Х	х	kh	as in Ba*ch* or Scottish lo*ch*.
Ц	ц	ts	as in le*ts*.
Ч	ч	ch	as in *ch*urch.
Ш	ш	sh	as in *sh*all.
Щ	щ	shch	as in fre*sh ch*eese.
	ъ	—	"hard sign" to indicate the preceding consonant is not palatalized. No distinct sound of its own.
	ы	ih	somewhat as in m*i*lk. There is no English equivalent for this sound. It is a short *i* pronounced at the back of the mouth.
	ь	y OR ^{y}	"soft sign" to indicate that the preceding consonant is palatalized. No distinct sound of its own.
Э	э	e OR eh	as in l*e*t.
Ю	ю	yoo	like the word *you*.
Я	я	yah	as in *ya*rd.

SOCIAL CONVERSATION

1. Good day.
Добрый день.
DAWB-rih‿y̆ dyen^{y}.

2. Good morning.
Доброе утро.
DAWB-ruh-yeh OOT-ruh.

3. Good evening.
Добрый вечер.
DAWB-rih‿y̆ VYEH-chehr.

4. Good night.
Спокойной ночи.
spah-KOY̆-nuh‿y̆ NAW-chee.

5. How do you do!
Здравствуйте!
ZDRAHST-voo‿y̆-tyeh.

6. Goodbye.
До свидания.
duh-sv^{y}ee-DAHN^{y}-yah.

7. Until next time.
Пока.
pah-KAH.

8. I want to see [Comrade Gvozdev].
Я хочу видеть [товарища Гвоздёва].
yah khah-CHOO V^{y}EE-dyet^{y} [tah-VAH-r^{y}ee-shchah gvahz-DYAW-vah].

9. —— Mr. Chernyshev.
господина Чернышёва.
gus-pah-D^{y}EE-nah chehr-nih-SHAW-vah.

10. —— Mrs. Popov.
Госпожу Попову.
gus-pah-ZHOO pah-PAW-voo.

11. Permit me to introduce you.
Позвольте вас познакомить.
pahz-VAWL^{y}-tyeh vahs puz-nah-KAW-m^{y}eet^{y}.

12. This is [Yevgheniy Nikolayevich Shcherbakov].
Это [Евгений Николаевич Щербаков].
EH-tuh [yev-GYEH-n^{y}ee‿y̆ n^{y}ee-kuh-LAH-yeh-v^{y}eech shcher-bah-KAWF].

13. —— my wife.
моя жена.
mah-YAH zheh-NAH,

14. —— my husband.
мой муж.
moy̆ moosh.

15. —— my mother.
моя мать.
mah-YAH maht^y.

16. —— my father.
мой отец.
moy̆ aht-YETS.

17. —— my daughter.
моя дочь.
mah-YAH dawch.

18. —— my son.
мой сын.
moy̆ sihn.

19. —— my sister.
моя сестра.
mah-YAH syest-RAH.

20. —— my brother.
мой брат.
moy̆ braht.

21. Pleased to meet you.
Очень приятно.
AW-chen^y pr^{y}ee-YAH-tnuh.

22. How are you?
Как вы поживаете?
kahk vih puh-zhee-VAH-yeh-tyeh?

23. Very well thanks, and you?
Очень хорошо, спасибо, а как вы?
AW-chen^y khuh-rah-SHAW, spah-S^{y}EE-buh, ah kahk vih?

24. All right.
Хорошо.
khuh-rah-SHAW.

25. How is your family?
Как ваша семья?
kahk VAH-shah syem^y-YAH?

26. Sit down please.
Садитесь пожалуйста.
sah-D^{y}EE-tyes^y pah-ZHAH-loo-stah.

27. It was very pleasant.
Было очень приятно.
BIH-luh AW-chen^y pr^{y}ee-YAH-tnuh.

28. Give my regards to your aunt and uncle.
Передайте привет вашим тёте и дяде.
pyeh-ryeh-DAH‿Y̆-tyeh pr^{y}ee-VYET VAH-sheem TYAW-tyeh ee DYAH-dyeh.

29. Come to see us again.
Приходите к нам опять.
pr^{y}ee-khah-D^{y}EE-tyeh k nahm ah-PYAHT^y.

30. What are you doing tonight?
Что вы делаете сегодня вечером?
shtaw vih DYEH-lah-yeh-tyeh syeh-VAW-dnyah VYEH-cheh-rum?

31. May I call on you again?
Можно придти к вам опять?
MAWZH-nuh pr^y^ee-T^y^EE k vahm ah-PYAHT^y^?

32. I like you very much.
Вы мне очень нравитесь.
vih mnyeh AW-chen^y^ NRAH-v^y^ee-tyes^y^.

33. Congratulations.
Поздравляю.
puz-drahv-LYAH-yoo.

34. Happy birthday.
Поздравляю с днём рожденья.
puz-drahv-LYAH-yoo s dnyawm rahzh-DYEN^y^-yah.

35. Happy New Year.
Счастливого нового года.
shchah-SL^y^EE-vuh-vuh NAW-vuh-vuh GAW-dah.

36. Merry Christmas.
Весёлого рождества.
vyeh-SYAW-luh-vuh ruzh-dyeh-STVAH.

PERSONAL MATTERS

37. What is your name?
Как ваше имя?
kahk VAH-sheh EE-myah?

38. My name is John.
Моё имя Джон.
mah-YAW EE-myah dzhawn.

39. I am 21 years old.
Мне двадцать один год.
mnyeh DVAH-tset^y^ ah-D^y^EEN gawt.

40. I am an American citizen.
Я американский гражданин *m*. (Я американская гражданка *f*.)
yah ah-myeh-r^y^ee-KAHN-sk^y^ee‿y̆ grahzh-dah-N^y^EEN m. (*yah ah-myeh-r^y^ee-KAHN-skah-yah grahzh-DAHN-kah* f.)

41. My mailing address is 920 Broadway, New York.
Мой почтовый адрес Бродвей, номер девятьсот двадцать, Нью Йорк.

moў pah-CHTAW-vih‿ў AHD-ryes "*Broadway*" *NAW-myehr dyeh-vyet^y-SAWT DVAHT-tset^y*, "*New York.*"

42. I am [a student].
Я [студент *m.* (студентка *f.*)].
yah [*stoo-DYENT* m. (*stoo-DYENT-kah* f.)].

43. —— a teacher.
преподаватель *m.* (преподавательница *f.*)
pryeh-puh-dah-VAH-tyel^y m. (*pryeh-puh-dah-VAH-tyel^y-n^{y}ee-tsah* f.)

44. —— an engineer.
инженер.
een-zheh-NYEHR.

45. —— a businessman.
коммерсант.
kuh-myehr-SAHNT.

46. —— a friend of Robert Brown.
друг *m.* Роберта Брауна.
drook m. *RAW-byehr-tah BROWN-ah.*

47. I am here [on vacation].
Я здесь [на время каникул].
yah zdyes^y [*nah VRYEH-myah kah-N^{y}EE-kool*].

48. —— on business.
по делу.
pah DYEH-loo.

49. I am traveling to Kuibyshev.
Я еду в Куйбышев.
yah YEH-doo f KOO‿Ў-bih-shef.

50. I am [warm].
Мне [тепло].
mnyeh [*tyep-LAW*].

51. —— cold.
холодно.
KHAW-lud-nuh.

52. —— thirsty.
хочется пить.
KHAW-cheh-tsah p^{y}eet^y.

53. —— hungry.
хочется есть.
KHAW-cheh-tsah yest^y.

54. I am [busy].
Я [занят *m.* (занята *f.*)].
yah [*ZAH-nyaht* m. (*zah-nyah-TAH* f.)].

55. —— tired.
устал *m.* (устала *f.*)
oo-STAHL m. (*oo-STAH-lah* f.)

MAKING YOURSELF UNDERSTOOD

56. Do you speak English?
Вы говорите по-английски?
vih guh-vah-R^{y}EE-tyeh puh-ahn-GL^{y}EE‿Ĭ-sk^{y}ee?

57. Does anyone here speak English?
Кто-нибудь здесь говорит по-английски?
KTAW-n^{y}ee-boot^{y} zdyes^{y} guh-vah-R^{y}EET puh-ahn-GL^{y}EE‿Ĭ-skee?

58. I read only English.
Я читаю только по-английски.
yah chee-TAH-yoo TAWL^{y}-kuh puh-ahn-GL^{y}EE‿Ĭ-sk^{y}ee.

59. I speak a little Russian.
Я говорю немного по-русски.
yah guh-vah-RYOO nyeh-MNAW-guh pah-ROOS-k^{y}ee.

60. Please speak more slowly.
Пожалуйста, говорите медленнее.
pah-ZHAH-loo-stah, guh-vah-R^{y}EE-tyeh MYED-lyen-yeh-yeh.

61. I do not understand.
Я не понимаю.
yah nyeh puh-n^{y}ee-MAH-yoo.

62. Do you understand me?
Вы понимаете меня?
vih puh-n^{y}ee-MAH-yeh-tyeh myeh-NYAH?

63. I do not know.
Я не знаю.
yah nyeh ZNAH-yoo.

64. I do not think so.
Я не думаю.
yah nyeh DOO-mah-yoo.

65. Repeat it, please.
Повторите, пожалуйста.
puf-tah-R^{y}EE-tyeh, pah-ZHAH-loo-stah.

66. Write it down please.
Напишите это, пожалуйста.
nah-p^{y}ee-SHEE-tyeh EH-tuh, pah-ZHAH-loo-stah.

67. What does this word mean?
Что значит это слово?
shtaw ZNAH-cheet EH-tuh SLAW-vuh?

68. What is this?
Что это?
shtaw EH-tuh?

69. How do you say "pen" in Russian?
Как сказать "pen" по-русски?
kahk skah-ZAHT^y "pen" pah-ROOS-k^{y}ee?

GENERAL EXPRESSIONS

70. Yes.
Да.
dah.

71. No.
Нет.
nyet.

72. Perhaps.
Может быть.
MAW-zhet biht^y.

73. Please.
Пожалуйста.
pah-ZHAH-loo-stah.

74. Excuse me.
Извините.
eez-v^{y}ee-N^{y}EE-tyeh.

75. Thanks very much.
Спасибо большое.
spah-S^{y}EE-buh bahl^y-SHAW-yeh.

76. You are welcome.
Пожалуйста.
pah-ZHAH-loo-stah.

77. All right.
Хорошо.
khuh-rah-SHAW.

78. Don't mention it.
Не стоит.
nyeh STAW-^{y}eet.

79. Very good.
Очень хорошо.
AW-chen^y khuh-rah-SHAW.

80. It is not important.
Это не важно.
EH-tuh nyeh VAHZH-nuh.

81. Do not bother, please.
Пожалуйста не беспокойтесь.
pah-ZHAH-loo-stah nyeh byes-pah-KOЎ-tyes^y.

82. Who are you?
Кто вы?
ktaw vih?

83. Who is [that boy]?
Кто [этот мальчик]?
ktaw [EH-tut MAHL^y-cheek]?

84. —— that young girl.
эта девушка.
EH-tah DYEH-voosh-kah.

85. —— that man.
этот мужчина.
EH-tut moo-SHCHEE-nah.

86. —— that woman.
эта женщина.
EH-tah ZHEN-shchee-nah.

87. Where can I wash my hands?
Где я могу помыть руки?
gdyeh yah mah-GOO pah-MIHT^y ROO-k^{y}ee?

88. Where is [the men's room]?
Где [мужская уборная]?
gdyeh [moosh SKAH-yah oo-BAWR-nah-yah]?

89. —— ladies' room.
женская уборная.
ZHEN-skah-yah oo-BAWR-nah-yah.

90. Why?
Почему?
puh-cheh-MOO?

91. How?
Как?
kahk?

92. What do you wish?
Что вы хотите?
shtaw vih khah-T^{y}EE-tyeh?

93. Come here!
Идите сюда!
ee-D^{y}EE-tyeh syoo-DAH!

94. Come in!
Войдите!
vah‿y̆-D^{y}EE-tyeh!

95. Wait a moment!
Подождите один момент!
puh-dah-ZHD^{y}EE-tyeh ah-D^{y}EEN mah-MYENT!

96. Not yet.
Нет ещё.
nyet yeh-SHCHAW.

97. Not now.
Не теперь.
nyeh tyeh-PYEHR^y.

98. Listen!
Послушайте!
pah-SLOO-shah‿y̆-tyeh!

99. Be careful!
Осторожно!
uh-stah-RAWZH-nuh!

DIFFICULTIES AND REPAIRS

100. Can you tell me?
Вы можете сказать мне?
vih MAW-zheh-tyeh skah-ZAHT^y mnyeh?

101. I am looking for my friends.
Я ищу своих друзей.
yah ee-SHCHOO svah-^yEEKH droo-ZYEŸ.

102. I cannot find my hotel address.
Я не могу найти адреса своего отеля.
yah nyeh mah-GOO nah‿ÿ-T^yEE AHD-ryeh-sah svuh-yeh-VAW ah-TEH-lyah.

103. She lost her handbag.
Она потеряла свою сумочку.
ah-NAH puh-tyeh-RYAH-lah svah-YOO SOO-much-koo.

104. He forgot [his money].
Он забыл [деньги].
awn zah-BIHL [DYEN^y-g^yee].

105. —— his wallet.
бумажник.
boo-MAHZH-n^yeek.

106. —— his keys.
ключи.
klyoo-CHEE.

107. What is the matter?
В чём дело?
f chawm DYEH-luh?

108. What am I to do?
Что мне делать?
shtaw mnyeh DYEH-laht^y?

109. My eyeglasses are broken.
Мои очки разбились.
mah-YEE ahch-K^yEE rahz-B^yEE-l^yees^y.

110. Ask at the lost-and-found bureau.
Обратитесь в бюро потерь и находок.
uh-brah-T^yEE-tyes^y v byoo-RAW pah-TYEHR^y ee nah-KHAW-duk.

111. The militia station.
Участок милиции.
oo-CHAH-stuk m^yee-L^yEE-tsee-^yee.

112. I shall call a militiaman.
Я позову милиционера.
yah puh-zah-VOO m^{y}ee-l^{y}ee-ts^{y}ee-ah-NYEH-rah.

113. The American Consulate.
Американское консульство.
ah-myeh-r^{y}ee-KAHN-skuh-yeh KAWN-sool^y-stvuh.

BAGGAGE

114. Where can we check our baggage through to Kerch?
Где мы можем сдать вещи в багаж для отправки в Керчь?
gdyeh mih MAW-zhem zdaht^y VYEH-shchee v bah-GAHZH dlyah aht-PRAHF-k^{y}ee f kyerch?

115. I want to leave these packages here for a few hours.
Я хочу оставить здесь эти пакеты на несколько часов.
yah khah-CHOO ah-STAH-v^{y}eet^y zdyes^y EH-t^{y}ee pah-KYEH-tih nah NYEH-skul^y-kuh chah-SAWF.

116. Handle this very carefully.
Обращайтесь с этим очень осторожно.
ah-brah-SHCHAH Ĭ-tyes^y s EH-t^{y}eem AW-chen^y ah-stuh-RAWZH-nuh.

CUSTOMS

117. Where is the customs office?
Где таможня?
gdyeh tah-MAWZH-nyah?

118. Here is [my baggage].
Вот [мой багаж].
vawt [moy̆ bah-GAHSH].

119. —— my passport.
мой паспорт.
moy̆ PAHS-purt.

120. —— my identification card.
моё удостоверение личности.
mah-YAW oo-duh-stuh-vyeh-RYEH-n^{y}ee-yeh L^{y}EECH-nuh-st^{y}ee.

121. —— my health certificate.
моё свидетельство о здоровье.
mah-YAW sv^{y}ee-DYEH-tyel^{y}-stvuh aw zdah-RAW-v^{y}yeh.

122. —— my visitor's visa.
моя виза туриста.
mah-YAH V^{y}EE-zah too-R^{y}EE-stah.

123. I am in transit.
Я еду транзитом.
yah YEH-doo trahn-Z^{y}EE-tum.

124. The bags over there are mine.
Чемоданы вон там мои.
cheh-mah-DAH-nih vawn tahm mah-YEE.

125. I have nothing to declare.
У меня ничего нет подлежащего пошлине.
oo myeh-NYAH n^{y}ee-cheh-VAW nyet pud-lyeh-ZHAH-shcheh-vuh PAWSH-l^{y}ee-nyeh.

126. All this is for my personal use.
Всё это для моего личного употребления.
vsyaw EH-tuh dlyah muh-yeh-VAW L^{y}EECH-nuh-vuh oo-puh-tryeb-LYEH-n^{y}ee-yah.

127. Is it necessary to open all the suitcases?
Нужно открыть все чемоданы?
NOOZH-nuh ut-KRIHT^{y} fsyeh cheh-mah-DAH-nih?

128. There is nothing here but clothing.
Здесь ничего нет кроме платья.
zdyes^{y} n^{y}ee-cheh-VAW nyet KRAW-myeh PLAHT^{y}-yah.

129. These are gifts.
Это подарки.
EH-tuh pah-DAHR-k^{y}ee.

130. Must duty be paid on these things?
Нужно платить пошлину на эти вещи?
NOOZH-nuh plah-T^{y}EET^{y} PAWSH-l^{y}ee-noo nah EH-t^{y}ee VYEH-shchee?

131. How much must I pay?
Сколько нужно заплатить?
SKAWL^{y}-kuh NOOZH-nuh zah-plah-T^{y}EET^{y}?

132. That is all I have.
Это всё, что у меня с собой.
EH-tuh fsyaw shtaw oo myeh-NYAH s sah-BOY̆.

133. Have you finished?
Вы кончили?
vih KAWN-chee-l^{y}ee?

TRAVEL DIRECTIONS

134. How do I get [to the airline office]?
Как мне пройти [в контору авиационной линии]?
kahk mnyeh prah‿y̆-T^{y}EE [f kahn-TAW-roo ah-v^{y}ee-ah-tsee-AWN-nuh‿y̆ L^{y}EE-n^{y}ee-^{y}ee]?

135. —— to the ticket reservation office.
в кассу предварительной продажи билетов.
f KAHS-soo pryed-vah-R^{y}EE-tyel^{y}-nuh‿y̆ prah-DAH-zhee b^{y}ee-LYEH-tuf.

136. —— to the Intourist Office.
в контору Интуриста.
f kahn-TAW-roo een-too-R^{y}EE-stah.

137. How long does it take to go to Archangel?
Сколько часов езды до Архангельска?
SKAWL^{y}-kuh chah-SAWF yez-DIH duh ahr-KHAHN-gyel^{y}-skah?

138. When will we arrive at Lake Ladoga?
Когда мы прибываем на Ладожское Озеро?
kahg-DAH mih pr^{y}ee-bih-VAH-yem nah LAH-dush-skuh-yeh AW-zveh-ruh?

139. Is this the direct way to Sochi?
Это прямой путь в Сочи?
EH-tuh pryah-MOY̆ poot^{y} f SAW-chee?

140. Please show me the way [to the business section].
Пожалуйста, покажите мне дорогу [в деловую часть города].
pah-ZHAH-loo-stah, puh-kah-ZHEE-tyeh mnyeh dah-RAW-goo [v dyeh-lah-VOO-yoo chahst^y GAW-ruh-dah].

141. —— to the residential section.
в жилую часть города.
v zhee-LOO-yoo chahst^y GAW-ruh-dah.

142. —— to the shopping section.
в часть города, где сосредоточены магазины.
f chahst^y GAW-ruh-dah, gdyeh sus-ryeh-dah-TAW-cheh-nih mah-gah-Z^{y}EE-nih.

143. —— to the city.
в центр города.
f tsentr GAW-ruh-dah.

144. —— to the village.
в деревню.
v dyeh-RYEV-nyoo.

145. —— out of town.
загород.
ZAH-guh-rut.

146. Do I turn [to the north]?
Мне следует повернуть [на север]?
mnyeh SLYEH-doo-yet puh-vyehr-NOOT^y [nah SYEH-vyehr]?

147. —— to the south.
на юг.
nah yook.

148. —— to the east.
на восток.
nah vah-STAWK.

149. —— to the west.
на запад.
nah ZAH-paht.

150. —— to the right.
направо.
nah-PRAH-vuh.

151. —— to the left.
налево.
nah-LYEH-vuh.

152. What street is this?
Какая это улица?
kah-KAH-yah EH-tuh OO-l^{y}ee-tsah?

153. Where is it?
Где это?
gdyeh EH-tuh?

154. How far is it?
Как далеко это?
kahk dah-lyeh-KAW EH-tuh?

155. Can I walk there?
Могу я пройти туда пешком?
mah-GOO yah prah‿ў-T^{y}EE too-DAH pyesh-KAWM?

156. Am I going in the right direction?
Я иду в правильном направлении?
yah ee-DOO f PRAH-v^{y}eel^y-num nah-prahv-LYEH-n^{y}ee-^{y}ee?

157. Should I go [this way]?
Нужно мне идти [в эту сторону]?
NOOZH-nah mnyeh ee-T^{y}EE [v EH-too STAW-ruh-noo]?

158. —— that way.
в ту сторону.
f too STAW-ruh-noo.

159. Is it [on this side of the street]?
Это [на этой стороне улицы]?
EH-tuh [nah EH-tuh‿ў stuh-rah-NYEH OO-l^{y}ee-tsih]?

160. —— on the other side of the street.
на другой стороне улицы.
nah droo-GOЎ stuh-rah-NYEH OO-l^{y}ee-tsih.

161. —— along the boulevard.
по бульвару.
pah bool^y-VAH-roo.

162. —— on the embankment.
на набережной.
nah NAH-byeh-ryezh-nuh‿ў.

163. —— across the bridge.
через мост.
CHEH-ryez mawst.

164. —— beyond the traffic light.
за светофором.
zah svyeh-tah-FAW-rum.

165. —— at the corner.
на углу.
nah oog-LOO.

166. —— in the middle.
посередине.
puh-syeh-ryeh-D^{y}EE-nyeh.

167. —— back.
позади.
puh-zah-D^{y}EE.

168. —— straight ahead.
впереди.
fpyeh-ryeh-D^{y}EE.

169. —— at the entrance.
у входа.
oo FKHAW-dah.

170. —— opposite the park.
против парка.
PRAW-t^{y}eef PAHR-kah.

171. —— beside the school.
рядом со школой.
RYAH-dum saw SHKAW-luh‿ÿ.

172. —— behind the building.
позади здания.
puh-zah-D^y^EE ZDAH-n^y^ee-yah.

173. —— down the stairs.
вниз по лестнице.
vn^y^ees pah LYEST-n^y^ee-tseh.

174. —— up the hill.
на горе.
nah gah-RYEH.

175. I am much obliged to you.
Я вам очень обязан *m.* (обязана *f.*)
yah vahm AW-chen^y^ ah-BYAH-zahn m. (*ah-BYAH-zah-nah* f.)

TICKETS

176. Where is [the ticket window]?
Где [билетная касса]?
gdyeh [b^y^ee-LYET-nah-yah KAHS-sah]?

177. —— the reservation window?
касса предварительной продажи билетов?
KAHS-sah pryed-vah-R^y^EE-tyel^y^-nuh‿ÿ prah-DAH-zhee b^y^ee-LYEH-tuf?

178. How much is [a round-trip ticket] to Kislovodsk?
Сколько стоит билет [туда и обратно] до Кисловодска?
SKAWL^y^-kuh STAW-^y^eet b^y^ee-LYET [too-DAH ee ahb-RAHT-nuh] dah k^y^ees-lah-VAWT-skah?

179. —— a one-way ticket.
в один конец.
v ah-D^y^EEN kah-NYETS.

180. —— a reserved-seat ticket.
Плацкарта.
plahts-KAHR-tah.

181. I have a reservation for this seat.
У меня плацкарта на это место.
oo myeh-NYAH plahts-KAHR-tah nah EH-tuh MYES-tuh.

182. May I stop at Yessentuki on the way?
Могу я прервать поездку в Ессентуках?
mah-GOO yah pryeh-RVAHT^{y} pah-YEST-koo v yes-syen-too-KAHKH?

183. First class.
Первый класс.
PYEHR-vih‿ў klahs.

184. Second class.
Второй класс.
ftah-ROЎ klahs.

185. Third class.
Третий класс.
TRYEH-t^{y}ee‿ў klahs.

186. Local train.
Пригородный поезд.
PR^{y}EE-guh-rud-nih‿ў PAW-yest.

187. Express train.
Экспресс.
eks-PRES.

BOAT

188. When must we go on board?
Когда мы должны быть на пароходе?
kahg-DAH mih dahl-ZHNIH biht^{y} nah pah-rah-KHAW-dyeh?

189. Bon Voyage!
Счастливого пути!
schah-STL^{y}EE-vuh-vuh poo-T^{y}EE!

190. Where is [the steward]?
Где [официант]?
gdyeh [uh-f^{y}ee-ts^{y}ee-AHNT]?

191. —— the cabin steward.
каютный.
kah-YOOT-nih‿ў.

192. —— the purser.
кассир.
kah-S^{y}EER.

193. —— the captain.
капитан.
kah-p^{y}ee-TAHN.

194. The dock.
Док.
dawk.

195. Cabin.
Каюта.
kah-YOO-tah.

196. The deck.
Палуба.
PAH-loo-bah.

AIRPLANE

197. I want [to make a plane reservation].
Я хочу [заказать место на аэроплане].
yah khah-CHOO [zah-kah-ZAHT^{y} MYES-tuh nah ah-eh-rah-PLAH-nyeh].

198. —— to confirm a plane reservation.
подтвердить свой заказ на место.
put-tvyehr-D^{y}EET^y svoў zah-KAHZ nah MYES-tuh.

199. Is there bus service between the hotel and the airport?
Есть ли автобусное сообщение между отелем и аэропортом?
yest^y l^{y}ee ahf-TAW-boos-nuh-yeh suh-ahp-SHCHEH-n^{y}ee-yeh myezh-DOO ah-TYEH-lyem ee ah-eh-rah-PAWR-tum?

200. At what time will they call for me?
В котором часу за мной заедут?
f kah-TAW-rum chah-SOO zah mnoў zah-YEH-doot?

201. Is flight twenty-three on time?
Полёт номер двадцать три не опаздывает?
pah-LYAWT NAW-myehr DVAH-tset^y tr^{y}ee nyeh uh-pahz-DIH-vah-yet?

202. How many kilos may I take?
Сколько кило можно взять с собой?
SKAWL^y-kuh k^{y}ee-LAW MAWZH-nuh vzyaht^y s sah-BOЎ?

203. How much do they charge per kilo for excess?
Сколько берут за кило сверх нормы?
SKAWL^y-kuh byeh-ROOT zah k^{y}ee-LAW svyerkh NAWR-mih?

TRAIN

204. Where is the railroad station?
Где вокзал?
gdyeh vahk-ZAHL?

205. When does the train for Dniepropetrovsk leave?
Когда отходит поезд в Днепропетровск?
kahg-DAH aht-KHAW-d^{y}eet PAW-yest v dnyeh-pruh-pyeh-TRAWVSK?

206. From what track does the train leave?
С какой платформы отходит поезд?
s kah-KOЙ plaht-FAWR-mih aht-KHAW-d^y eet PAW-yest?

207. Please open the window.
Пожалуйста откройте окно.
pah-zhah-LOO-stah aht-KROЙ-tyeh ahk-NAW.

208. Close the door.
Закройте дверь.
zah-KROЙ-tyeh dvyehr^y.

209. Where is [the diner]?
Где [вагон-ресторан]?
gdyeh [vah-GAWN-ryeh-stah-RAHN]?

210. —— the sleeper.
спальный вагон.
SPAHL^y-nih‿й vah-GAWN.

211. —— the smoking car.
вагон для курящих.
vah-GAWN dlyah koo-RYAH-shcheekh.

212. Where are we now?
Где мы теперь?
gdyeh mih tyeh-PYEHR^y?

213. Is smoking permitted here?
Можно здесь курить?
MAWZH-nuh zdyes^y koo-R^yEET^y?

BUS, STREETCAR AND SUBWAY

214. What streetcar goes to the Park of Culture and Rest?
Какой трамвай идёт в Парк Культуры и Отдыха?
kah-KOЙ trahm-VAH‿Й ee-DYAWT f pahrk kool^y-TOO-rih ee AWT-dih-khah?

215. Where is the bus stop?
Где остановка автобуса?
gdyeh us-tah-NAWF-kah ahf-TAW-boo-sah?

216. Can I take this subway line to the University?
Можно доехать до университета по этой линии метро?
MAWZH-nuh dah-YEH-khaht[y] daw oo-n[y]ee-vyehr-s[y]ee-TYEH-tah pah EH-tuh‿ў L[y]EE-n[y]ee-[y]ee myeh-TRAW?

217. Do I have to change?
Нужно пересаживаться?
NOOZH-nuh pyeh-ryeh-SAH-zhee-vah-tsah?

218. A transfer, please.
Билет с пересадкой, пожалуйста.
b[y]ee-LYET s pyeh-ryeh-SAHT-kuh‿ў, pah-ZHAH-loo-stah.

219. Conductor, please tell me where I must get off.
Кондуктор, пожалуйста скажите, где мне сойти.
kahn-DOOK-tur, pah-ZHAH-loo-stah skah-ZHEE-tyeh, gdyeh mnyeh sah‿ў-T[y]EE.

TAXI

220. Please call a taxi for me.
Пожалуйста вызовите мне такси.
pah-ZHAH-loo-stah VIH-zuh-v[y]ee-tyeh mnyeh tahk-S[y]EE.

221. Is the taxi free?
Такси свободно?
tahk-S[y]EE svah-BAWD-nuh?

222. What do you charge [per hour]?
Сколько вы берёте [за час]?
SKAWL[y]-kuh vih byeh-RYAW-tyeh [zah chahs]?

223. —— per kilometer.
за километр.
zah k[y]ee-lah-MYETR.

224. Please drive [more slowly].
Пожалуйста поезжайте [медленнее].
pah-ZHAH-loo-stah puh-yez-ZHAH‿ў-tyeh [MYED-lyen-nyeh-yeh].

225. —— more carefully.
осторожнее.
uh-stah-RAWZH-nyeh-yeh.

226. Stop here.
Остановитесь здесь.
uh-stah-nah-V^{y}EE-tyes^{y} zdyes^{y}.

227. Wait for me.
Подождите меня.
puh-dah-ZHD^{y}EE-tyeh myeh-NYAH.

AUTOMOBILE TRAVEL

228. Where can I rent a car?
Где я могу взять автомобиль на прокат?
gdyeh yah mah-GOO vzyaht^{y} ahf-tuh-mah-B^{y}EEL^{y} nah prah-KAHT?

229. I have [an international driver's license].
У меня [международное шофёрское свидетельство].
oo myeh-NYAH [myezh-doo-nah-RAWD-nuh-yeh shah-FYAWR-skuh-yeh sv^{y}ee-DYEH-tyel^{y}-stvuh].

230. —— a credit card.
кредитная карточка.
kryeh-D^{y}EET-nah-yah KAHR-tuch-kah.

231. A gas station.
Заправочный пункт.
zah-PRAH-vuch-nih‿ў poonkt.

232. A mechanic.
Механик.
myeh-KHAH-n^{y}eek.

233. Is the road [good]?
Дорога [хорошая]?
dah-RAW-guh [khah-RAW-shah-yah]?

234. —— rough.
плохая.
plah-KHAH-yah.

235. Where does that road lead?
Куда ведёт эта дорога?
koo-DAH vyeh-DYAWT EH-tah dah-RAW-gah?

236. What town is this?
Какой это город?
kah-KOЎ EH-tuh GAW-rut?

237. And the next one?
А следующий?
ah SLYEH-doo-yoo-shchee‿ў?

238. Can you show it to me on the map?
Можете вы показать мне его на карте?
MAW-zheh-tyeh vih puh-kah-ZAHT^{y} mnyeh yeh-VAW nah KAHR-tyeh?

239. Give me forty liters.
Дайте мне сорок литров.
DAH‿Ĭ-tyeh mnyeh SAW-ruk L^{y}EET-ruf.

240. Check the oil.
Проверьте масло.
prah-VYEHR^{y}-tyeh MAHS-luh.

241. Put water in the radiator.
Налейте воды в радиатор.
nah-LYEĬ-tyeh vah-DIH v rah-d^{y}ee-AH-tur.

242. Lubricate the car.
Смажьте машину.
SMAHSH-tyeh mah-SHEE-noo.

243. Charge the battery.
Зарядите батарею.
zah-ryah-D^{y}EE-tyeh bah-tah-RYEH-yoo.

244. Adjust the brakes.
Наладьте тормоза.
nah-LAHT^{y}-tyeh tur-mah-ZAH.

245. Can you check the tires?
Можете вы проверить шины?
MAW-zheh-tyeh vih prah-VYEH-r^{y}eet^{y} SHEE-nih?

246. Can you repair this flat tire now?
Можете вы починить эту сдавшую шину сейчас же?
MAW-zheh-tyeh vih puh-chee-N^{y}EET^{y} EH-too SDAHV-shoo-yoo SHEE-noo syeĭ-CHAHS zheh?

247. The engine overheats.
Мотор перегревается.
mah-TAWR pyeh-ryeh-gryeh-VAH-yeh-tsah.

248. The motor [misses] stalls.
Мотор [даёт перебои] глохнет.
mah-TAWR [dah-YAWT pyeh-ryeh-BAW-ee] GLAWKH-nyet.

249. The windshield wiper does not work.
Стеклоочиститель не работает.
styek-luh-ahchee-ST^{y}EE-tyel^y nyeh rah-BAW-tah-yet.

250. May I park here for a while?
Можно мне поставить здесь машину на время?
MAWZH-nuh mnyeh pah-STAH-v^{y}eet^y zdyes^y mah-SHEE-noo nah VRYEH-myah?

HOTEL AND APARTMENT

251. I am looking for [a good hotel].
Я ищу [хороший отель].
yah ee-SHCHOO [khah-RAW-shee‿ÿ ah-TEL^y].

252. —— an inexpensive hotel.
недорогую гостиницу.
nyeh-duh-rah-GOO-yoo gah-ST^{y}EE-n^{y}ee-tsoo.

253. —— a furnished room.
мебелированную комнату.
myeh-byeh-l^{y}ee-RAW-vahn-noo-yoo KAWM-nah-too.

254. I have [a hotel reservation].
У меня [заказан номер].
oo myeh-NYAH [zah-KAH-zahn NAW-myehr].

255. Do you have a room free?
У вас есть свободные номера?
oo vahs yest^y svah-BAWD-nih-yeh nuh-myeh-RAH?

256. Do you have [a single room]?
У вас найдётся [комната]?
oo vahs nah‿ÿ-DYAW-tsah [KAWM-nah-tah]?

257. —— a double room.
для двоих.
dlyah dvah-^{y}EEKH.

258. —— a two-or three-room suite.
двух или трёхкомнатный номер.
dvookh EE-l^{y}ee tryawkh-KAWM-naht-nih‿ÿ NAW-myehr.

259. Is there a safe deposit box in the hotel?
Есть ли сейф при отеле?
yest^y l^{y}ee s^{y}eў̆f pr^{y}ee ah-TYEH-lyeh?

260. I want a room [with a double bed].
Мне нужна комната [с двухспальной кроватью].
mnyeh noozh-NAH KAWM-nah-tah [s dvookh-SPAHL^y-nuh‿ў̆ krah-VAHT^y-yoo].

261. —— with twin beds.
с двумя кроватями.
s dvoo-MYAH krah-VAH-tyah-m^{y}ee.

262. —— with a bath.
с ванной.
s VAHN-nuh‿ў̆.

263. —— with a shower.
с душем.
s DOO-shem.

264. I am looking for a room, [without meals].
Я ищу комнату, [без стола].
yah ee-SHCHOO KAWM-nah-too, [byes stah-LAH].

265. —— for tonight.
на сегодня.
nah syeh-VAW-dnyah.

266. —— for several days.
на несколько дней.
nah NYEH-skawl^y-kuh dnyeў̆.

267. —— for two persons.
для двоих.
dlyah dvah-^{y}EEKH.

268. I should like to see the room.
Я хотел бы посмотреть комнату.
yah khah-TYEL bih puh-smah-TRYET^y KAWM-nah-too.

269. Is it [upstairs]?
Она [наверху]?
ah-NAH [nah-vyehr-KHOO]?

270. —— downstairs.
внизу.
vn^{y}ee-ZOO.

271. Is there an elevator?
Есть ли лифт?
yest^y l^{y}ee l^{y}eeft?

272. Room service, please.
Бюро обслуживания, пожалуйста.
byoo-RAW ahb-SLOO-zhee-vah-n^{y}*ee-yah, pah-ZHAH-loo-stah.*

273. Please send a porter to my room at once.
Пожалуйста пошлите в мой номер человека за багажом сейчас же.
pah-ZHAH-loo-stah pah-SHL^{y}*EE-tyeh v moў NAW-myehr cheh-lah-VYEH-kah zah bah-gah-ZHAWM syeў-CHAHS zheh.*

274. —— a chambermaid.
уборщицу.
oo-BAWR-shchee-tsoo.

275. Please wake me at a quarter past nine o'clock.
Пожалуйста разбудите меня четверть десятого.
pah-ZHAH-loo-stah rahz-boo-D^{y}*EE-tyeh myeh-NYAH CHET-vyehrt*^{y} *dyeh-SYAH-tuh-vuh.*

276. Do not disturb me until then.
Не беспокойте меня до тех пор.
nyeh byes-pah-KOЎ-tyeh myeh-NYAH dah tyekh pawr.

277. We should like to have breakfast in our room.
Мы хотели бы завтракать у себя в номере.
mih khah-TYEH-l^{y}*ee-bih ZAHF-trah-kaht*^{y} *oo syeh-BYAH v NAW-myeh-ryeh.*

278. Who is it?
Кто это?
ktaw EH-tuh?

279. Come back later.
Придите позже.
pr^{y}*ee-D*^{y}*EE-tyeh PAW-zheh.*

280. I need [a blanket].
Мне нужно [одеяло].
mnyeh NOOZH-nuh [uh-dyeh-YAH-luh].

281. Bring me [a pillow].
Принесите мне [подушку].
pr^{y}*ee-nyeh-S*^{y}*EE-tyeh mnyeh [pah-DOOSH-koo].*

282. —— a pillowcase.
наволочку.
NAH-vuh-luch-koo.

283. —— toilet paper.
бумагу для уборной.
boo-MAH-goo dlyah oo-BAWR-nuh‿y̆.

284. —— sheets.
простыни.
PRAW-stih-n^{y}ee.

285. —— a bath mat.
ванный коврик.
VAHN-nih‿y̆ KAWV-r^{y}eek.

286. —— soap.
мыло.
MIH-luh.

287. —— towels.
полотенца.
puh-lah-TYEN-tsah.

288. —— coat hangers.
вешалки для платья.
VYEH-shahl-k^{y}ee dlyah PLAHT^y-yah.

289. I should like to speak to the manager.
Я хотел *m.* (хотела *f.*) бы поговорить с управляющим.
yah khah-TYEL m. (*khah-TYEH-lah* f.) *bih puh-guh-vah-R^{y}EET^y s oo-prah-VLYAH-yoo-shcheem.*

290. My room key, please.
Ключ от моего номера, пожалуйста.
klyooch ut muh-yeh-VAW NAW-myeh-rah, pah-ZHAH-loo-stah.

291. Are there any letters for me?
Есть ли для меня письма?
yest^y l^{y}ee dlyah myeh-NYAH P^{y}EES^y-mah?

292. What is my room number?
Какой мой номер?
kah-KOY̆ moy̆ NAW-myehr?

293. I am leaving at ten o'clock.
Я уезжаю в десять часов.
yah oo-yezh-ZHAH-yoo v DYEH-syet^y chah-SAWF.

294. Please make out my bill as soon as possible.
Пожалуйста приготовьте мой счёт как можно скорее.
pah-ZHAH-loo-stah pr^y ee-gah-TAWF^y-tyeh moў shchawt kahk MAWZH-nuh skah-RYEH-yeh.

295. Is the service charge included?
Включено ли обслуживание?
fklyoo-cheh-NAW l^y ee ahp-SLOO-zhee-vah-n^y ee-yeh?

296. Please forward my mail to American Express in Paris.
Мои письма перешлите, пожалуйста, Американскому Экспрессу в Париж.
mah-YEE PEES^y-mah pyeh-ryeh-SHL^y EE-tyeh, pah-ZHAH-loo-stah, ah-myeh-r^y ee-KAHN-skuh-moo eks-PREH-soo f pah-R^y EESH.

CONVERSATION ON THE TELEPHONE

297. Междугороднюю, пожалуйста.
myezh-doo-gah-RAWD-nyoo-yoo, pah-ZHAH-loo-stah.
Long distance, please.

298. Сию минуту.
S^y EE-yoo m^y ee-NOO-too.
One minute.

299. Алло! Междугородняя? Я хочу говорить с Ленинградом, Кировская подстанция два-семьдесят три-пятьдесят шесть.
ahl-LAW! myezh-doo-gah-RAWD-nyah-yah? yah khah-CHOO guh-vah-R^y EET^y s lyeh-n^y een-GRAH-dum, K^y EE-ruf-skah-yah paht-STAHN-ts^y ee-yah, dvah-SYEM^y-dyeh-syet tr^y ee-pyaht^y-dyeh-SYAHT shest^y.
Hello! Long distance? I want to speak with Leningrad, Kirovskaya, 2-73-56.

300. Ваш номер телефона?
vahsh NAW-myehr tyeh-lyeh-FAW-nah?
Your telephone number?

301. Мой номер Загородная подстанция 4-97-81. Сколько стоит трёхминутный разговор?
moй NAW-myehr ZAH-guh-rud-nah-yah pahd-STAHN-tsʸee-yah cheh-TIH-ryeh dyeh-vyeh-NAW-stuh syemʸ, VAW-syemʸ-dyeh-syet ah-dʸeen. SKAWLʸ-kuh STAW-ʸeet tryawkh mʸee-NOOT-nih‿ÿ rahz-gah-VAWR?
My number is Zagorodnaya 4-97-81. What is the charge for a three-minute call?

302. Двенадцать рублей шестьдесят пять копеек. Свыше трёх минут — восемь рублей сорок копеек. Соединяю с Ленинградом. Говорите.
dveh-NAH-tsahtʸ roob-LYEŸ shestʸ-dyeh-SYAHT pyahtʸ kah-PYEH-yek. SVIH-sheh tryawkh mʸee-NOOT — VAW-syemʸ roob-LYEŸ SAW-ruk kah-PYEH-yek. suh-yeh-dee-NYAH-yoo s lyeh-nʸeen-GRAH-dum. guh-vah-RʸEE-tyeh.
12 rubles 65 kopeks. Over three minutes—8 rubles 40 kopeks. I am connecting you. Speak!

303. Алло! Говорит Глеб Александрович Глинка. Могу я говорить с товарищем Журавлёвым?
ahl-LAW! guh-vah-RʸEET glyep ah-lyeh-KSAHN-druh-v eech GLEENK-ah. mah-GOOH yah guh-vah-RʸEETʸ s tah-VAH-rʸee-shchem zhoo-rahv-LYAW-vihm?
Hello! Gleb Alexandrovich Glinka speaking. May I speak to comrade Zhuravlev?

304. Сожалению его нет дома и он вернётся не раньше пол десятого вечера.
suh-zhah-LYEH-nee-yoo yeh-VAW nyet DAW-mah ee awn vyehr-NYAW-tsah nyeh RAHNʸ-sheh pawl dyeh-SYAH-tuh-vuh VYEH-cheh-rah.
I am sorry he isn't in and he won't be back until 9.30 this evening.

305. Можете вы передать ему кое-что? Скажите ему, пожалуйста, что звонил Глеб Александрович Глинка. Я буду в Ленинграде в воскресенье. Пусть он позвонит мне в воскресенье утром до двенадцати. Я остановлюсь в отеле "Астория," телефон Центральная 3-45-70, комната № 602.
MAW-zheh-tyeh vih pyeh-ryeh-DAHTʸ yeh-MOO KAW-yeh shtaw? skah-ZHEE-tyeh yeh-MOO, pah-ZHAH-loo-stah, shtaw zvah-NʸEEL glyep ah-lyeh-

KSAHN-druh-veech GLEENK-ah. yah BOO-doo v lyeh-n^{y}een-GRAH-dyeh v vuh-skryeh-SYEN^{y}-yeh. poost^{y} awn pah-zvah-N^{y}EET mnyeh v vuh-skryeh-SYEN^{y}-yeh OOT-rum daw dvyeh-NAH-tsah-t^{y}ee. yah uh-stah-nahv-LYOO^{y}S v ah-TYEH-lyeh ''ah-STAW-r^{y}ee-yah'', tyeh-lyeh-FAWN tsen-TRAHL^{y}-nah-yah tr^{y}ee SAW-ruk pyaht^{y} SYEM^{y}-dyeh-syaht, KAWM-nah-tah NAW-myehr shest^{y}-SAWT dvah.

Can you give him a message? Please tell him that Gleb Alexandrovich Glinka called. I will be in Leningrad on Sunday. He can telephone me Sunday morning before 12. I shall stay at the Astoria Hotel, telephone Central 3-45-70, room 602.

306. Так. Я записала. Что-нибудь ещё?
tahk. yah zah-p^{y}ee-SAH-lah. SHTAW-n^{y}ee-boot^{y} yeh-SHCHAW?
O.K. I have written it down. Anything else?

307. Нет, это всё, благодарю вас. Извините за беспокойство.
nyet, EH-tuh fsyaw, bluh-guh-dah-RYOO vahs. eez-v^{y}ee-N^{y}EE-tyeh zah byes-pah-KOY̆-stvuh.
No, that is all, thank you. Sorry to have troubled you.

308. Пожалуйста, никакого беспокойства. Я передам ему что вы сказали.
pah-ZHAH-loo-stah, n^{y}ee-kah-KAW-vuh byes-pah-KOY̆-stvah. yah pyeh-ryeh-DAHM yeh-MOO shtaw vih skah-ZAH-l^{y}ee.
No trouble at all. I shall give your message to him.

309. Большое спасибо. До свидания.
bahl^{y}-SHAW-yeh spah-S^{y}EE-buh. duh-sv^{y}ee-DAHN^{y}-yah.
Many thanks. Goodbye.

310. До свидания.
duh-sv^{y}ee-DAHN^{y}-yah.
Goodbye.

AT THE BAR

311. I should like to have [some vodka].
Я хотел *m.* (хотела *f.*) бы выпить [водки]
yah khah-TYEL m. (*khah-TYEH-lah* f.) *bih VIH-p^{y}eet^y* [*VAWT-k^{y}ee*].

312. —— a glass of sherry.
рюмку "шерри".
RYOOM-koo SHEHR-r^{y}ee.

313. —— a mug of beer.
кружку пива.
KROOSH-koo P^{y}EE-vah.

314. —— wine.
вина.
v^{y}ee-NAH.

315. —— a bottle of mineral water.
бутылку минеральной воды.
boo-TIHL-koo m^{y}ee-nyeh-RAHL^y-nuh‿y̆ vah-DIH.

316. Let's have another.
Выпьем ещё по одной.
VIH-p^{y}yem yeh-SHCHAW pah ahd-NOY̆.

317. To your health.
За ваше здоровье.
zah VAH-sheh zdah-RAWV^y-yeh.

AT THE RESTAURANT

318. Can you recommend a good restaurant?
Можете ли вы порекомендовать мне хороший ресторан?
MAW-zheh-tyeh l^{y}ee vih puh-ryeh-kuh-myen-dah-VAHT^y mnyeh khah-RAW-shee‿y̆ ryes-tah-RAHN?

319. Where can I have [breakfast]?
Где я могу [позавтракать]?
gdyeh yah mah-GOO [*pah-ZAHF-trah-kaht^y*]?

320. —— lunch.
покушать среди дня.
pah-KOO-shaht^y sryeh-D^{y}EE dnyah.

321. —— snack.
перекусить.
pyeh-ryeh-koo-S[y]EET[y].

322. —— dinner.
пообедать.
puh-ah-BYEH-daht[y].

323. At what time is supper served?
В котором часу подают ужин?
f kah-TAW-rum chah-SOO puh-dah-YOOT OO-zheen?

324. Are you [my waiter]?
Вы [мой официант]?
vih moў [uh-f[y]ee-tsee-AHNT]?

325. —— my waitress.
моя официантка.
mah-YAH uh-f[y]ee-tsee-AHNT-kah.

326. A table for two by the window, if possible.
Столик для двоих у окна, если можно.
STAW-l[y]eek dlyah dvah-YEEKH oo ahk-NAH, YES-l[y]ee MAWZH-nuh.

327. Bring me [the menu].
Принесите мне [меню].
pr[y]ee-nyeh-S[y]EE-tyeh mnyeh [myeh-NYOO].

328. —— the wine list.
карту вин.
KAHR-too v[y]een.

329. —— a napkin.
салфетку.
sahl-FYET-koo.

330. —— a fork.
вилку.
V[y]EEL-koo.

331. —— a knife.
нож.
nawsh.

332. —— a plate.
тарелку.
tah-RYEL-koo.

333. —— a teaspoon.
чайную ложку.
CHAH‿Ў-noo-yoo LAWSH-koo.

334. —— a tablespoon.
столовую ложку.
stah-LAW-voo-yoo LAWSH-koo.

335. I want to order something [plain].
Я хочу заказать что-нибудь [простое].
yah khah-CHOO zah-kah-ZAHT^{y} SHTAW-n^{y}ee-boot^{y} [prah-STAW-yeh].

336. —— not too spicy.
не слишком острое.
nyeh SL^{y}EESH-kum AWST-ruh-yeh.

337. —— not too sweet.
не слишком сладкое.
nyeh SL^{y}EESH-kum SLAHT-kuh-yeh.

338. —— not too fat.
не слишком жирное.
nyeh SL^{y}EESH-kum ZHEER-nuh-yeh.

339. —— fried.
жареное.
ZHAH-ryeh-nuh-yeh.

340. —— boiled.
варёное.
vah-RYAW-nuh-yeh.

341. I like the meat [rare].
Я люблю мясо [недожареное].
yah lyoob-LYOO MYAH-suh [nyeh-dah-ZHAH-ryeh-nuh-yeh].

342. —— medium.
средней готовности.
SRYED-n^{y}eў gah-TAWV-nuh-st^{y}ee.

343. —— well done.
хорошо прожареное.
khuh-rah-SHAW prah-ZHAH-ryeh-nuh-yeh.

344. A little more.
Ещё немного.
yeh-SHCHAW nyeh-MNAW-guh.

345. A little less.
Немного меньше.
nyeh-MNAW-guh MYEN^{y}-sheh.

346. Enough, thank you.
Довольно, спасибо.
dah-VAWL^{y}-nuh, spah-S^{y}EE-buh.

347. I did not order this.
Я этого не заказывал *m.* (заказывала *f.*)
yah EH-tuh-vuh nyeh zah-KAH-zih-vahl m. (*zah-KAH-zih-vah-lah* f.)

348. May I change this for a salad?
Можно переменить это на салат?
MAWZH-nuh pyeh-ryeh-myeh-N^y^EET^y^ EH-tuh nah sah-LAHT?

349. The bill, please.
Счёт, пожалуйста.
shchawt, pah-ZHAH-loo-stah.

350. Is the tip included?
Чаевые включены?
chah-yeh-VIH-yeh fklyoo-cheh-NIH?

351. There is a mistake in the bill.
В счёте ошибка.
f SHCHAW-tyeh ah-SHEEP-kah.

352. What is this for?
За что это?
zah shtaw EH-tuh?

353. Keep the change.
Сдачу оставьте себе.
ZDAH-choo ah-STAHF^y^-tyeh syeh-BYEH.

354. The food and service were excellent.
Еда и обслуживание были замечательными.
yeh-DAH ee ahp-SLOO-zhee-vah-n^y^ee-yeh BIH-l^y^ee zah-myeh-CHAH-tyel^y^-nih-m^y^ee.

355. Hearty appetite!
Приятного аппетита!
pr^y^ee-YAHT-nuh-vuh ah-pyeh-T^y^EE-tah!

FOOD LIST

356. Please bring me some water [with ice].
Пожалуйста принесите мне воды [со льдом].
pah-ZHAH-loo-stah pr^y^ee-nyeh-S^y^EE-tyeh mnyeh vah-DIH [sah l^y^dawm].

357. —— without ice.
безо льда.
BYEH-zuh l^y^dah.

358. Please pass [the bread].
Пожалуйста передайте [хлеб].
pah-ZHAH-loo-stah pyeh-ryeh-DAH‿Y̆-tyeh [khlyep].

359. —— the rolls.
булочки.
BOO-luch-k^{y}ee.

360. —— the butter.
масло.
MAHS-luh.

361. —— the sugar.
сахар.
SAH-khahr.

362. —— the salt.
соль.
sawl^y.

363. —— the pepper.
перец.
PYEH-ryets.

364. —— vegetable oil.
растительное масло.
rah-ST^{y}EE-tyel^y-nuh-yeh MAHS-luh.

365. —— the vinegar.
уксус.
OOK-soos.

366. —— the garlic.
чеснок.
ches-NAWK.

367. —— the mustard.
горчицу.
gahr-CHEE-tsoo.

368. —— mayonnaise.
майонез.
mah‿ў-ah-NEZ.

369. —— gravy.
подливку.
pahd-L^{y}EEF-koo.

370. —— the sauce.
соус.
SAW-oos.

BREAKFAST FOODS

371. May I have [some fruit juice]?
Могу я получить [какой-нибудь фруктовый сок]?
mah-GOO yah puh-loo-CHEET^y [kah-KOЎ-n^{y}ee-BOOT^y frook-TAW-vih‿ў sawk]?

372. —— orange juice.
апельсинный сок.
ah-pyel^y-S^{y}EEN-nih‿ў sawk.

373. —— tomato juice.
томатный сок.
tah-MAHT-nih‿ў sawk.

374. —— cooked cereal.
какую-нибудь кашу.
kah-KOO-yoo-n^{y}ee-BOOT^y KAH-shoo.

375. —— oatmeal.
овсянку.
ahf-SYAHN-koo.

376. —— **toast and jam.**
поджареный хлеб и джем.
pahd-ZHAH-ryeh-nih‿y̆ khlyep ee dzhem.

377. —— **honey.**
мёд.
myawt.

378. —— **an omelet.**
омлет.
ahm-LYET.

379. —— **soft-boiled eggs.**
яйца всмятку.
YAH‿Y̆-tsah FSMYAHT-koo.

380. —— **hard-boiled eggs.**
яйца вкрутую.
YAH‿Y̆-tsah fkroo-TOO-yoo.

381. —— **fried eggs.**
яичницу.
yah-ʸEESH-nʸee-tsoo.

382. —— **scrambled eggs.**
яичницу болтунью.
yah-ʸEESH-nʸee-tsoo bahl-TOONʸ-yoo.

ENTRÉES

383. **I want to order [some chicken soup].**
Я хочу заказать [куриный суп].
yah kah CHOO zah-kah-ZAHTʸ [koo-RʸEE-nih‿y̆ soop].

384. —— **vegetable soup.**
овощной суп.
uh-vahshch-NOY̆ soop.

385. —— **beef.**
говядину.
gah-VYAH-dʸee-noo.

386. —— **roast beef.**
ростбиф.
RAWST-bʸeef.

387. —— **roast chicken.**
жареного цыплёнка.
ZHAH-ryeh-nuh-vuh tsihp-LYAWN-kah.

388. —— **duck.**
утку.
OOT-koo.

389. —— **fish.**
рыбу.
RIH-boo.

390. —— **goose.**
гуся.
GOO-syah.

391. —— **lamb.**
баранину.
bah-RAH-n^{y}ee-noo.

392. —— **liver.**
печёнку.
pyeh-CHAWN-koo.

393. —— **lobster.**
омара.
ah-MAH-rah.

394. —— **oysters.**
устриц.
OO-str^{y}eets.

395. —— **pork.**
свинину.
sv^{y}ee-N^{y}EE-noo.

396. —— **sardines.**
сардинки.
sahr-D^{y}EEN-k^{y}ee.

397. —— **sausage.**
колбасу.
kul-bah-SOO.

398. —— **steak.**
бифштекс.
b^{y}eef-SHTEKS.

399. —— **veal.**
телятину.
tyeh-LYAH-t^{y}ee-noo.

VEGETABLES AND SALADS

400. I want to order [some asparagus].
Я хочу заказать [спаржу].
yah khah-CHOO zah-kah-ZAHT^y [SPAHR-zhoo].

401. —— **beans.**
фасоль.
fah-SAWL^y.

402. —— **cabbage.**
капусту.
kah-POO-stoo.

403. —— **carrots.**
морковь.
mahr-KAWF^y.

404. —— **cauliflower.**
цветную капусту.
tsvyet-NOO-yoo kah-POO-stoo.

405. —— **cucumbers.**
огурцы.
uh-goor-TSIH.

406. —— **lettuce.**
зелёный салат.
zyeh-LYAW-nih‿y̆ sah-LAHT.

407. —— **mushrooms.**
грибы.
gr^{y}ee-BIH.

408. —— **onions.**
лук.
look.

409. —— **green peas.**
зелёный горошек.
zyeh-LYAW-nih‿y̆ gah-RAW-shek.

410. —— **green peppers.**
зелёный перец.
zyeh-LYAW-nih‿y̆ PYEH-ryets.

411. —— **boiled potatoes.**
отварной картофель.
ut-vahr-NOY̆ kahr-TAW-fyel^{y}*.*

412. —— **mashed potatoes.**
картофельное пюре.
kahr-TAW-fyel^{y}*-nuh-yeh pyoo-RYEH.*

413. —— **rice.**
рис.
r^{y}*ees.*

414. —— **spinach.**
шпинат.
shp^{y}*ee-NAHT.*

415. —— **tomatoes.**
помидоры.
puh-m^{y}*ee-DAW-rih.*

FRUITS

416. Do you have [apples]?
У вас есть [яблоки]?
oo vas yest^{y} *[YAH-bluh-k*^{y}*ee]?*

417. —— **cherries.**
вишни.
V^{y}*EESH-n*^{y}*ee.*

418. —— **grapes.**
виноград.
v^{y}*ee-nah-GRAHT.*

419. —— **lemons.**
лимоны.
l^{y}*ee-MAW-nih.*

420. —— **melon.**
дыня.
DIH-nyah.

421. —— **oranges.**
апельсины.
ah-pyel^{y}*-S*^{y}*EE-nih.*

422. —— **peaches.**
персики.
PYEHR-s^{y}*ee-k*^{y}*ee.*

423. —— **raspberries.**
малина.
mah-L^{y}*EE-nah.*

424. —— **strawberries.**
земляника.
zyem-lyah-N^{y}*EE-kah.*

BEVERAGES

425. I want [a cup of black coffee].
Я хочу [чашку чёрного кофе].
yah khah-CHOO [CHAHSH-koo CHAWR-nuh-vuh KAW-fyeh].

426. —— **coffee with cream.**
кофе со сливками.
KAW-fyeh sah SL^{y}EEF-kah-m^{y}ee.

427. —— **a glass of milk.**
стакан молока.
stah-KAHN muh-lah-KAH.

428. —— **tea.**
чаю.
CHAH-yoo.

429. —— **lemonade.**
лимонаду.
l^{y}ee-mah-NAH-doo,

430. —— **soda water with fruit syrup.**
газированной воды с сиропом.
gah-z^{y}ee-RAW-vahn-nuh‿y̆ vah-DIH s s^{y}ee-RAW-pum.

DESSERTS

431. **I want to have [some cake].**
Я хочу взять [кусок торта].
yah khah-CHOO vzyaht^y [koo-SAWK TAWR-tah].

432. —— **a piece of pie.**
кусок пирога.
koo-SAWK p^{y}ee-rah-GAH.

433. —— **a small cake.**
пирожное.
p^{y}ee-RAWZH-nuh-yeh.

434. —— **cookies.**
печенье.
pyeh-CHEN^y-yeh.

435. —— **cheese.**
сыру.
SIH-roo.

436. —— **chocolate ice cream.**
шоколадное мороженое.
shuh-kah-LAHD-nuh-yeh mah-RAW-zheh-nuh-yeh.

437. —— **vanilla ice cream.**
сливочное мороженое.
SL^{y}EE-vuch-nuh-yeh mah-RAW-zheh-nuh-yeh.

CONVERSATION AT THE POST OFFICE

438. Я хотел бы послать это письмо в Соединённые Штаты. Сколько это будет стоить?
yah khah-TYEL bih pah-SLAHT^{y} EH-tuh p^{y}ees^{y}-MAW f suh-yeh-d^{y}ee-NYAWN-nih-yeh SHTAH-tih. SKAWL^{y}-kuh EH-tuh BOO-dyet STAW-^{y}eet^{y}?
I should like to send this letter to the United States. How much will the postage cost?

439. Обычной почтой — сорок копеек, воздушной почтой — рубль сорок.
ah-BIHCH-noy̆ PAWCH-tuh‿y̆ SAW-ruk kah-PYEH-yek, vahz-DOOSH-noy̆ PAWCH-tuh‿y̆ roobl^{y} SAW-ruk.
By regular mail—40 kopeks, by airmail 1 ruble 40 kopeks.

440. Воздушной почтой, пожалуйста. Дайте мне шесть марок по десять копеек, три марки по пятнадцать копеек, и одну марку за тридцать три копейки.
vahz-DOOSH-nuh‿y̆ PAWCH-tuh‿y̆, pah-ZHAH-loo-stah. DAH‿Y̆-tyeh mnyeh shest^{y} MAH-ruk pah DYEH-syet^{y} kah-PYEH-yek, tr^{y}ee MAHR-kee pah pyet-NAH-tsaht^{y} kah-PYEH-yek, ee ahd-NOO MAHR-koo zah TR^{y}EE-tset^{y} tr^{y}ee kah-PEY̆-k^{y}ee.
By airmail, please. Give me 6 ten-kopek stamps, 3 fifteen-kopek stamps, and a 33-kopek stamp.

441. Вот ваши марки. Всего два рубля девяносто восемь копеек. Письмо опустите в почтовый ящик "Письма заграницу."
vawt VAH-shee MAHR-k^{y}ee. fsyeh-VAW dvah roob-LYAH dyeh-vyeh-NAW-stuh VAW-syem^{y} kah-PYEH-yek. p^{y}ees^{y}-MAW uh-poo-ST^{y}EE-tyeh f pahch-TAW-vih‿y̆ YAH-shcheek "PEES^{y}-mah zah-grah-N^{y}EE-tsoo".
Here are your stamps. That will be 2 rubles 98 kopeks. Drop your letter in the mailbox "letters abroad".

442. Благодарю вас. Как я могу послать посылку в Соединённые Штаты?
blah-guh-dah-RYOO vahs. kahk yah mah-GOO pah-SLAHT[y] pah-SIHL-koo f suh-yeh-d[y]ee-NYAWN-nih-yeh SHTAH-tih?
Thank you. How can I send a package to the United States?

443. Заполните этот бланк на посылку и сдайте его вместе с посылкой у соседнего окна направо.
zah-PAWL-n[y]ee-tyeh EH-tut blahnk nah pah-SIHL-koo ee SDAH‿Ў-tyeh yeh-VAW VMYEH-styeh s pah-SIHL-kuh‿ў oo sah-SYED-nyeh-vuh ahk-NAH nah-PRAH-vuh.
Fill out this parcel post form and hand it in together with your package at the next window to the right.

444. Можно застраховать посылку?
MAWZH-nuh zah-strah-khah-VAHT[y] pah-SIHL-koo?
May I insure the package?

445. Да. Укажите сумму страховки в бланке. Что в посылке?
dah. oo-kah-ZHEE-tyeh SOOM-moo strah-KHAWF-k[y]ee v BLAHN-kyeh. shtaw f pah-SIHL-kyeh?
Yes. You indicate the amount of insurance on the form. What does the package contain?

446. Только грелка на чайник. Ничего бьющегося.
TAWL[y]-kuh GRYEL-kah nah CHAH‿Ў-n[y]eek, n[y]ee-cheh-VAW BYOO-shcheh-vuh-syah.
Only a tea cozy, nothing fragile.

447. Четыре рубля восемьдесят копеек. Вот ваша квитанция.
cheh-TIH-ryeh roob-LYAH VAW-syem[y]-dyeh-set kah-PYEH-yek. vawt VAH-shah kvee-TAHN-tsee-yah.
4 rubles and 80 kopeks. Here is your receipt.

448. Спасибо.
spah-S[y]EE-buh.
Thank you.

CHURCH

449. Is there an English-speaking priest here?
Есть ли здесь священник, говорящий по-английски?
yest^y l^{y}ee zdyes^y svyah-SHCHEN-n^{y}eek guh-vah-RYAH-shchee‿y̆ puh-ahn-GL^{y}EE‿Y̆-sk^{y}ee?

450. —— a minister.
пастор.
PAH-stur.

451. —— a rabbi.
раввин.
rahv-V^{y}EEN.

452. A Catholic church.
Католическая церковь.
kah-tah-L^{y}EE-ches-kah-yah TSEHR-kuf^y.

453. A Protestant church.
Протестантская церковь.
pruh-tyeh-STAHNT-skah-yah TSEHR-kuf^y.

454. A Russian Orthodox church.
Русская православная церковь.
ROOS-kah-yah prah-vah-SLAHV-nah-yah TSEHR-kawf^y.

455. A synagogue.
Синагога.
s^{y}ee-nah-GAW-gah.

456. When is the service in the church?
Когда служба в церкви?
kahg-DAH SLOOZH-bah f TSEHRK-v^{y}ee?

SIGHTSEEING

457. We want a licensed guide who speaks English.
Нам нужен официальный гид, говорящий по-английски.
nahm NOO-zhen uh-f^{y}ee-tsee-AHL^y-nih‿y̆ g^{y}eed, guh-vah-RYAH-shchee‿y̆ puh-ahn-GL^{y}EE‿Y̆-sk^{y}ee.

458. What is the charge [per hour]?
Сколько это стоит [в час]?
SKAWL^y-kuh EH-tuh STAW-^{y}eet [f chahs]?

459. —— per day.
в день.
v dyen^y.

460. I am interested [in architecture].
Меня интересует [архитектура].
myeh-NYAH een-tyeh-ryeh-SOO-yet [ahr-kh^{y}ee-tyek-TOO-rah].

461. —— in painting.
живопись.
ZHEE-vuh-p^{y}ees^y.

462. —— in sculpture.
скульптура.
skool^{y}p-TOO-rah.

463. Show us [the most important sights].
Покажите нам [самые выдающиеся достопримечательности].
puh-kah-ZHEE-tyeh nahm [SAH-mih-yeh vih-dah-YOO-shchee-yeh-syah duh-stuh-pr^{y}ee-myeh-CHAH-tyel^y-nuh-st^{y}ee].

464. —— the cathedral.
собор.
sah-BAWR.

465. —— the museum.
музей.
moo-ZYEЎ.

466. When does it [open]?
Когда здесь [открывается]?
kahg-DAH zdyes^y [ut-krih-VAH-yeh-tsah]?

467. —— close.
закрывается.
zah-krih-VAH-yeh-tsah.

468. Where is [the entrance]?
Где здесь [вход]?
gdyeh zdyes^y [fkhawt]?

469. —— the exit.
выход.
VIH-khut.

AMUSEMENTS

470. I should like to go [to a concert].
Я хотел *m.* (хотела *f.*) бы пойти [на концерт].
yah khah-TYEL m. *(khah-TYEH-lah* f.) *bih pah‿ў-T^{y}EE [nah kahn-TSEHRT].*

471. —— to a matinée.
на дневное представление.
nah dnyev-NAW-yeh pryet-stahv-LYEH-n^{y}ee-yeh.

472. —— to the movies.
в кино.
f k^{y}ee-NAW.

473. —— to a variety show.
в театр-варьете.
f tyeh-AHTR-vahr^{y}-YEH-teh.

474. —— to the circus.
в цирк.
f tseerk.

475. —— to the opera.
в оперу.
v AW-pyeh-roo.

476. —— to the ballet.
на балет.
nah bah-LYET.

477. —— to the Bolshoi Theater.
в Большой Театр.
v bahl^{y}-SHOY̆ tyeh-AHTR.

478. —— to the box office.
в кассу театра.
f KAHS-soo tyeh-AH-trah.

479. What is playing tonight?
Что идёт сегодня?
shtaw ee-DYAWT syeh-VAW-dnyah?

400. When does it begin?
Когда начало?
kahg-DAH nah-CHAH-luh?

481. How much is the admission charge?
Какая входная плата?
kah-KAH-yah fkhahd-NAH-yah PLAH-tah?

482. Have you seats [in the orchestra] for tonight?
Есть ли места [в партере] на сегодня?
yest^{y} l^{y}ee myeh-STAH [f pahr-T^{y}EH-ryeh] nah syeh-VAW-dnyah?

483. —— in the balcony.
на балконе.
nah bahl-KAW-nyeh.

484. —— in a box.
в ложе.
v LAW-zheh.

485. Can I see and hear well from there?
Оттуда хорошо видно и слышно?
aht-TOO-dah khuh-rah-SHAW VʸEED-nuh ee SLIHSH-nuh?

486. When does the intermission begin?
Когда начнётся антракт?
kahg-DAH nahch-NYAW-tsah ahn-TRAHKT?

487. Where can we go to dance?
Куда мы можем пойти потанцовать?
koo-DAH mih MAW-zhem pah‿y̆-TʸEE puh-tahn-tsah-VAHTʸ?

488. May I have this dance?
Разрешите пригласить вас на этот танец?
rahz-ryeh-SHEE-tyeh prʸee-glah-SʸEETʸ vahs nah EH-tut TAH-nyets?

SPORTS

489. Let's go [to the beach].
Давайте поедем [на пляж].
dah-VAH‿Y̆-tyeh pah-YEH-dyem [nah plyahsh].

490. —— to a soccer game.
на футбольный матч.
nah foot-BAWLʸ-nih‿y̆ mahtch.

491. —— to the races.
на скачки.
nah SKAHCH-kʸee.

492. —— to the swimming pool.
в плавательный бассейн.
f PLAH-vah-tyelʸ-nih‿y̆ bahs-SYEY̆N.

493. Can we go [fishing]?
Можно нам поехать [ловить рыбу]?
MAWZH-nuh nahm pah-YEH-khahtʸ [lah-VʸEETʸ RIH-boo]?

494. —— horseback riding.
кататься верхом.
kah-TAH-tsah vyehr-KHAWM.

495. —— skating.
кататься на коньках.
kah-TAH-tsah nah kahn^{y}*-KAHKH.*

496. —— skiing.
кататься на лыжах.
kah-TAH-tsah nah LIH-zhahkh.

497. —— swimming.
плавать.
PLAH-vaht^{y}*.*

BANK AND MONEY

498. Where can I change foreign money?
Где я могу обменять иностранную валюту?
gdyeh yah mah-GOO ub-myeh-NYAHT^{y} *ee-nah-STRAHN-noo-yoo vah-LYOO-too?*

499. Where is the bank?
Где банк?
gdyeh bahnk?

500. Will you accept [my personal check]?
Вы примете [мой личный чек]?
vih PR^{y}*EE-myeh-tyeh [moy̆ L*^{y}*EECH-nih‿y̆ chek]?*

501. —— a traveler's check.
путевой чек.
poo-tyeh-VOY̆ chek.

502. What is the exchange rate on the dollar today?
Какой курс доллара сегодня?
kah-KOY̆ koors DAWL-lah-rah syeh-VAW-dnyah?

503. Can you change fifty dollars into rubles?
Вы можете обменять мне пятьдесят долларов на рубли?
vih MAW-zheh-tyeh ub-myeh-NYAHT^{y} *mnyeh pyet*^{y}*-dyeh-SYAHT DAWL-lah-ruf nah roob-L*^{y}*EE?*

504. Please give me [some large bills].
Пожалуйста дайте мне [крупными деньгами].
pah-ZHAH-loo-stah DAH‿Ĭ-tyeh mnyeh [KROOP-nih-m^{y}ee dyen^{y}-GAH-m^{y}ee].

505. —— some small bills.
мелкими деньгами.
MYEL-k^{y}ee-m^{y}ee dyen^{y}-GAH-m^{y}ee.

506. —— some change.
немного мелочи.
nyeh-MNAW-guh MYEH-luh-chee.

SHOPPING

507. I want to go shopping.
Я хочу пойти за покупками.
yah khah-CHOO pah‿y̆-T^{y}EE zah pah-KOOP-kah-m^{y}ee.

508. What do you wish?
Что вы желаете?
shtaw vih zheh-LAH-yeh-tyeh?

509. I do not like this one.
Мне это не нравится.
mnyeh EH-tuh nyeh NRAH-v^{y}ee-tsah.

510. How much does this cost?
Сколько это стоит?
SKAWL^{y}-kuh EH-tuh STAW-^{y}eet?

511. The price is ten rubles and eighty-seven kopeks.
Цена десять рублей восемьдесят семь копеек.
tseh-NAH DYEH-syet^{y} roob-LYEĬ VAW-syem^{y}-dyeh-syet syem^{y} kah-PYEH-yek.

512. I want something [better].
Я хочу что-нибудь [получше].
yah khah-CHOO SHTAW-nee-boot^{y} [pah-LOOCH-sheh].

513. —— cheaper.
подешевле.
puh-dyeh-SHEV-lyeh.

514. —— larger.
побольше.
pah-BAWL^y-sheh.

515. —— smaller.
поменьше.
pah-MYEN^y-sheh.

516. —— stronger.
посильнее.
puh-s^{y}eel^y-NYEH-yeh.

517. May I try this on?
Можно мне это примерить?
MAWZH-nuh mnyeh EH-tuh pr^{y}ee-MYEH-r^{y}eet^y?

518. Can I order the same thing in another size?
Могу я заказать точно такое другого размера?
mah-GOO yah zah-kah-ZAHT^y TAWCH-nuh tah-KAW-yeh droo-GAW-vuh rahz-MYEH-rah?

519. Please take the measurements.
Пожалуйста снимите мерку.
pah-ZHAH-loo-stah sn^{y}ee-M^{y}EE-tyeh MYEHR-koo.

520. The length and width.
Длина и ширина.
dl^{y}ee-NAH ee shee-r^{y}ee-NAH.

521. How much time do you need to make it?
Сколько времени нужно чтобы это сделать?
SKAWL^y-kuh VRYEH-myeh-n^{y}ee NOOZH-nuh SHTAW-bih EH-tuh SDYEH-laht^y?

522. I'll return a little later.
Я вернусь через некоторое время.
yah vyehr-NOOS^y CHEH-ryez NYEH-kuh-tuh-ruh-yeh VRYEH-myah.

523. Can you ship it to New York?
Можете ли вы отправить это в Нью Йорк?
MAW-zheh-tyeh lee vih aht-PRAH-v^{y}eet^y EH-tuh f "New York"?

524. Do I pay [the salesgirl]?
Платить [продавщице]?
plah-T^{y}EET^y [pruh-dahf-SHCHEE-tseh]?

525. —— the salesman.
продавцу.
pruh-dahf-TSOO.

526. Please give me a bill for all the purchases.
Пожалуйста дайте мне чек на все покупки.
pah-ZHAH-loo-stah DAH‿Ĭ-tyeh mnyeh chek nah fsyeh pah-KOOP-kʸee.

527. Please wrap it carefully for export.
Пожалуйста упакуйте хорошенько для отправки.
pah-ZHAH-loo-stah oo-pah-KOO‿Ĭ-tyeh khuh-rah-SHENʸ-kuh dlyah aht-PRAHF-kʸee.

CLOTHING

528. I want to buy [a bathing cap].
Я хочу купить [купальный чепчик].
yah khah-CHOO koo-PʸEETʸ [koo-PHALʸ-nih‿ў CHEP-cheek].

529. —— a bathing suit.
купальный костюм.
koo-PAHLʸ-nih‿ў kahs-TYOOM.

530. —— a brassiere.
лифчик.
LʸEEF-cheek.

531. —— an overcoat.
пальто.
pahlʸ-TAW.

532. —— a dress.
платье.
PLAHTʸ-yeh.

533. —— a pair of galoshes.
пару галош.
PAH-roo gah-LAWSH.

534. —— a pair of gloves.
пару перчаток.
PAH-roo pyehr-CHAH-tuk.

535. —— a handbag.
сумочку.
SOO-much-koo.

536. —— a hat.
шляпу.
SHLYAH-poo.

537. —— a jacket.
жакет.
zhah-KYET.

538. —— underwear (men's).
мужское бельё.
moosh-SKAW-yeh byelʸ-YAW.

539. —— a nightgown.
ночную рубашку.
nahch-NOO-yoo roo-BAHSH-koo.

540. —— a raincoat.
дождевой плащ.
duzh-dyeh-VOЙ plahshch.

541. —— a pair of ladies' shoes.
пару туфель.
PAH-roo TOO-fyel^y.

542. —— a pair of men's shoes.
пару ботинок.
PAH-roo bah-T^{y}EE-nuk.

543. —— some shoelaces.
шнурки для ботинок.
shnoor-K^{y}EE dlyah bah-T^{y}EE-nuk.

544. —— a skirt.
юбку.
YOOP-koo.

545. —— a pair of house slippers.
пару домашних туфель.
PAH-roo dah-MAHSH-n^{y}eekh TOO-fyel^y.

546. —— a shirt.
рубашку.
roo-BAHSH-koo.

547. —— a pair of socks.
пару носков.
PAH-roo nahs-KAWF.

548. a pair of nylon stockings.
пару капроновых чулок.
PAH-roo kah-PRAW-nuh-vihkh choo-LAWK.

549. —— a suit.
костюм.
kahs-TYOOM.

550. —— a woolen sweater.
шерстяной светер.
shehr-styah-NOЙ SVYEH-tehr.

551. —— some neckties.
галстуки.
GAHL-stoo-k^{y}ee.

552. —— a pair of trousers.
пару брюк.
PAH-roo bryook.

553. a coat (suit).
пиджак.
p^{y}ee-DZHAHK.

COLORS

554. Show me [a lighter shade].
Покажите мне [более светлый оттенок].
puh-kah-ZHʸEE-tyeh mnyeh [BAW-lyeh-yeh SVYET-lih‿ÿ aht-TYEH-nuk].

555. —— a darker shade.
более тёмный оттенок.
BAW-lyeh-yeh TYAWM-nih‿ÿ aht-TYEH-nuk.

556. Black.
Чёрный.
CHAWR-nih‿ÿ.

557. Blue.
Голубой.
guh-loo-BOЎ.

558. Dark blue.
Синий.
Sʸ EE-nʸee‿ÿ.

559. Brown.
Коричневый.
kah-RʸEECH-nyeh-vih‿ÿ.

560. Gray.
Серый.
SYEH-rih‿ÿ.

561. Green.
Зелёный.
zyeh-LYAW-nih‿ÿ.

562. Orange.
Оранжевый.
ah-RAHN-zheh-vih‿ÿ.

563. Pink.
Розовый.
RAW-zuh-vih‿ÿ.

564. Purple.
Фиолетовый.
fʸee-ah-LYEH-tuh-vih‿ÿ.

565. Red.
Красный.
KRAHS-nih‿ÿ.

566. White.
Белый.
BYEH-lih‿ÿ.

567. Yellow.
Жёлтый.
ZHAWL-tih‿ÿ.

STORES

568. Where can I find [a bakery]?
Где я смогу найти [хлебную лавку]?
gdyeh yah smah-GOO nah‿ÿ-TʸEE [KHLYEB-noo-yoo LAHF-koo]?

569. —— a candy and pastry store.
кондитерскую.
kahn-DʸEE-tyehr-skoo-yoo.

570. —— a ready-to-wear clothing store.
магазин готового платья.
mah-gah-ZʸEEN gah-TAW-vuh-vuh PLAHTʸ-yah.

571. —— a department store.
универмаг.
oo-nʸee-vyehr-MAHK.

572. —— a grocery store.
бакалейную лавку.
bah-kah-LYEЎ-noo-yoo LAHF-koo.

573. —— a hardware store.
скобяную лавку.
skuh-byah-NOO-yoo LAHF-koo.

574. —— a jewelry store.
ювелирный магазин.
yoo-vyeh-LʸEER-nih‿ў mah-gah-ZʸEEN.

575. —— a marketplace.
рынок.
RIH-nuk.

576. —— a meat market.
мясной рынок.
myahs-NOЎ RIH-nuk.

577. —— a shoe store.
обувной магазин.
uh-boov-NOЎ mah-gah-ZʸEEN.

578. —— a tailor.
портного.
pahrt-NAW-vuh.

BOOKSTORE AND STATIONER'S

579. Where is there [a bookstore]?
Где здесь [книжный магазин]?
gdyeh zdyesʸ [KNʸEEZH-nih‿ў mah-gah-ZʸEEN]?

580. —— a stationer's.
писчебумажный магазин.
pʸee-shcheh-boo-MAHZH-nih‿ў mah-gah-ZʸEEN.

581. —— a newsstand.
газетный киоск.
gah-ZYET-nih‿y̆ k^{y}ee-AWSK.

582. I want to buy [a book].
Я хочу купить [книгу].
yah khah-CHOO koo-P^{y}EET^y [KN^{y}EE-goo].

583. —— a guidebook.
путеводитель.
poo-tyeh-vah-D^{y}EE-tyel^y.

584. —— a dictionary.
словарь.
slah-VAHR^y.

585. —— a magazine.
журнал.
zhoor-NAHL.

586. —— a newspaper.
газету.
gah-ZYEH-too.

587. —— a map of the Soviet Union.
карту Советского Союза.
KAHR-too sah-VYET-skuh-vuh sah-YOO-zah.

588. I need some [envelopes].
Мне нужны [конверты].
mnyeh noozh-NIH [kahn-VYEHR-tih].

589. —— postcards.
почтовые открытки.
pahch-TAW-vih-yeh aht-KRIHT-k^{y}ee.

590. I need a pencil.
Мне нужен карандаш.
mnyeh NOO-zhen kah-rahn-DAHSH.

591. I need a fountain pen.
Мне нужно вечное перо.
mnyeh NOOZH-nuh VYECH-nuh-yeh pyeh-RAW.

592. I need some writing paper.
Мне нужна почтовая бумага.
mnyeh noozh-NAH pahch-TAW-vah-yah boo-MAH-gah.

CIGAR STORE

593. Where is the nearest cigar store?
Где здесь ближайшая табачная лавка?
gdyeh zdyes^{y} bl^{y}ee-ZHAH‿Ĭ-shah-yah tah-BAHCH-nah-yah LAHF-kah?

594. What kind of cigars do you have?
Какие у вас есть сигары?
kah-K^{y}EE-yeh oo vahs yest^{y} s^{y}ee-GAH-rih?

595. I want to buy [a pack of American cigarettes].
Я хочу купить [пачку американских папирос].
yah khah-CHOO koo-P^{y}EET^{y} [PAHCH-koo ah-myeh-r^{y}ee-KAHN-sk^{y}eekh pah-p^{y}ee-RAWS].

596. —— a lighter.
зажигалку.
zah-zhee-GAHL-koo.

597. —— some pipe tobacco.
табаку для трубки.
tah-bah-KOO dlyah TROOP-k^{y}ee.

598. Do you have a match?
У вас найдётся спичка?
oo vahs nah‿y̆-DYAW-tsah SP^{y}EECH-kah?

CAMERA STORE

599. I want a roll of film for this camera.
Мне нужна катушка плёнки вот для этого фото-аппарата.
mnyeh noozh-NAH kah-TOOSH-kah PLYAWN-k^{y}ee vawt dlyah EH-tuh-vuh FAW-tuh-ah-pah-RAH-tah.

600. How much do you charge for developing color films?
Сколько вы берёте за проявление цветной плёнки?
SKAWL-kuh vih byeh-RYAW-tyeh zah pruh-yahv-LYEH-n^{y}ee-yeh tsvyet-NOĬ PLYAWN-k^{y}ee?

601. When will they be ready?
Когда будет готово?
kahg-DAH BOO-dyet gah-TAW-vuh?

602. May I take a snapshot of you?
Можно мне вас сфотографировать?
MAWZH-nuh mnyeh vahs sfuh-tuh-grah-F^y^EE-ruh-vaht^y^?

PHARMACY

603. Do you know a pharmacy where they speak English?
Знаете вы аптеку, где говорят по-английски?
ZNAH-yeh-tyeh vih ahp-TYEH-koo, gdyeh guh-vah-RYAHT puh-ahn-GL^y^EE‿Ĭ-sk^y^ee?

604. Do you have some aspirin?
У вас есть аспирин?
oo vahs yest^y^ ahs-p^y^ee-R^y^EEN?

605. I want to speak to [a male clerk].
Я хочу поговорить с [продавцом].
yah khah-CHOO puh-guh-vah-R^y^EET^y^ s [pruh-dahf-TSAWM].

606. —— a female clerk.
продавщицей.
pruh-dahf-SHCHEE-tseў.

607. Can you fill this prescription immediately?
Вы сможете приготовить мне этот рецепт немедленно?
vih SMAW-zheh-tyeh pr^y^ee-gah-TAW-v^y^eet^y^ mnyeh EH-tut ryeh-TSEPT nyeh-MYED-lyen-nuh?

608. I shall wait.
Я подожду.
yah puh-dah-ZHDOO.

LAUNDRY AND DRY CLEANING

609. Where is [the laundry] here?
Где здесь [прачечная]?
gdyeh zdyes^y^ [PRAH-chesh-nah-yah]?

610. —— the dry-cleaning service.
химическая чистка.
khʸee-Mʸ EE-cheh-skah-yah CHEEST-kah.

611. These shirts must be washed and mended.
Эти рубашки нужно выстирать и заштопать.
EH-tee roo-BAHSH-kʸee NOOZH-nuh VIH-stʸee-rahtʸ ee zah-SHTAW-pahtʸ.

612. Do not starch.
Не крахмальте.
nyeh krahkh-MAHLʸ-tyeh.

613. This suit must be cleaned and pressed.
Этот костюм нужно вычистить и выгладить.
EH-tut kahs-TYOOM NOOZH-nuh VIH-chees-tʸeetʸ ee VIH-glah-dʸeetʸ.

614. The belt is missing.
Не хватает пояса.
nyeh khvah-TAH-yet PAW-yah-sah.

615. Can you [sew on this button]?
Можете вы [пришить мне эту пуговицу]?
MAW-zheh-tyeh vih [prʸee-SHEETʸ mnyeh EH-too POO-guh-vʸee-tsoo]?

616. —— put in a new zipper.
вставить новую застёжку молнию.
FSTAH-veetʸ NAW-voo-yoo zah-STYAWSH-KOO MAWL-nʸee-yoo.

BARBER SHOP AND BEAUTY SALON

617. Where is there [a hairdresser]?
Где здесь [дамская парикмахерская]?
gdyeh zdyesʸ [DAHM-skah-yah pah-rʸeek-MAH-khyehr-skah-yah]?

618. —— a barber shop.
мужская парикмахерская.
moosh-SKAH-yah pah-rʸeek-MAH-khyehr-skah-yah.

619. —— a beauty salon.
косметический кабинет.
kus-myeh-T^y EE-cheh-sk^y ee‿ў KAH-b^y ee-nyet.

620. A haircut, please.
Постричь, пожалуйста.
pah-STR^y EECH, pah-ZHAH-loo-stah.

621. Not too short.
Не слишком коротко.
nyeh SL^y EESH-kum KAW-rut-kuh.

622. Give me a shave, please.
Побрейте меня, пожалуйста.
pah-BRYEЎ-tyeh myeh-NYAH, pah-ZHAH-loo-stah.

623. Wash my hair.
Вымойте мне голову.
VIH-moў-tyeh mnyeh GAW-luh-voo.

624. Set my hair.
Уложите мне волосы.
oo-luh-ZHEE-tyeh mnyeh VAW-luh-sih.

625. Give me a [permanent] please.
Сделайте мне [перманент] пожалуйста.
ZDYEH-lah‿ў-tyeh mnyeh [pyehr-mah-NYENT] pah-ZHAH-loo-stah.

626. —— a facial.
массаж лица.
mahs-SAHZH l^y ee-TSAH.

627. —— a manicure.
маникюр.
mah-n^y ee-KYOOR.

HEALTH AND ILLNESS

628. I want to go to see an American doctor.
Я хочу пойти к американскому доктору.
yah khah-CHOO pah‿ў-T^y EE k ah-myeh-r^y ee-KAHN-skuh-moo DAWK-tuh-roo.

629. Is the doctor in?
Доктор принимает?
DAWK-tur pr^y ee-n^y ee-MAH-yet?

630. I have [a headache].
У меня болит [голова].
oo myeh-NYAH bah-LYEET [guh-lah-VAH].

631. —— a sore throat.
горло.
GAWR-luh.

632. I have [a cold].
У меня [простуда].
oo myeh-NYAH [prah-STOO-dah].

633. —— a cough.
кашель.
KAH-shel^y.

634. —— a fever.
лихорадка.
l^{y}ee-khah-RAHT-kah.

635. —— nausea.
тошнота.
tush-nah-TAH.

636. —— constipation.
запор.
zah-PAWR.

637. —— diarrhea.
понос.
pah-NAWS.

638. —— indigestion.
расстройство желудка.
rahs-STROЎ-stvuh zheh-LOOT-kah.

639. —— pain in my chest.
боль в груди.
BAWL^y v groo-D^{y}EE.

640. There is something in my eye.
Мне что-то попало в глаз.
mnyeh SHTAW-tuh pah-PAH-luh v glahs.

641. I sleep poorly.
Я плохо сплю.
yah PLAW-khuh splyoo.

642. How do you feel?
Как вы себя чувствуете?
kahk vih syeh-BYAH CHOO-stvoo-yeh-tyeh?

643. I feel [well].
Я чувствую себя [хорошо].
yah CHOO-stvoo-yoo syeh-BYAH [khuh-rah-SHAW].

644. —— better.
лучше.
LOOCH-sheh.

645. —— worse.
хуже.
KHOO-zheh.

646. Must I stay in bed?
Мне нужно лежать в кровати?
mnyeh NOOZH-nuh lyeh-ZHAHT^y f krah-VAH-t^{y}ee?

647. When shall I be able to continue my trip?
Когда я смогу продолжать поездку?
kahg-DAH yah smah-GOO pruh-dahl-ZHAHT^y puh-YEZT-koo?

DENTIST

648. Do you know a good dentist?
Вы знаете хорошего зубного врача?
vih ZNAH-yeh-tyeh khah-RAW-sheh-vuh zoob-NAW-vuh vrah-CHAH?

649. This tooth hurts.
У меня болит этот зуб.
oo myeh-NYAH bah-L^{y}EET EH-tut zoop.

650. I seem to have lost the filling.
Я, кажется, потерял *m.* (потеряла *f.*) пломбу.
yah, KAH-zheh-tsah, puh-tyeh-RYAL m. (*puh-tyeh-RYAH-lah* f.) *PLAWM-boo.*

651. Can you fix it temporarily?
Сможете ли вы подлечить его на время?
SMAW-zheh-tyeh l^{y}ee vih pud-lyeh-CHEET^y yeh-VAW nah VRYEH-myah?

652. I do not want you to pull it out.
Я не хочу, что бы вы его вырвали.
yah nyeh khah-CHOO shtaw bih vih yeh-VAW VIHR-vah-l^{y}ee.

TIME

653. What time is it?
Который час?
kah-TAW-rih‿ў chahs?

654. It is very early.
Очень рано.
AW-chen^y RAH-nuh.

655. It is too late.
Слишком поздно.
SL^{y}EESH-kum PAWZ-nuh.

656. It is almost two o'clock A.M. (P.M.)*
Почти два часа. (Четырнадцать часов).
pah-CHT^y^EE dvah chah-SAH. (cheh-TIHR-nah-tsaht^y^ chah-SAWF).

657. It is half past three.
Половина четвёртого.
puh-lah-V^y^EE-nah chet-VYAWR-tuh-vuh.

658. It is a quarter past four.
Четверть пятого.
CHET-vyehrt^y^ PYAH-tuh-vuh.

659. It is a quarter to five.
Без четверти пять.
byez CHET-vyehr-t^y^ee pyaht^y^.

660. Ten to six.
Без десяти шесть.
byez dyeh-syeh-T^y^EE shest^y^.

661. At twenty minutes past seven.
В двадцать минут восмого.
v DVAH-tset^y^ m^y^ee-NOOT vahs^y^-MAW-vuh.

662. In the morning.
Утром.
OOT-rum.

663. In the afternoon.
Днём.
dnyawm.

664. In the evening.
Вечером.
VYEH-cheh-rum.

665. Last year. В прошлом году.
f PRAWSH-lum gah-DOO.

666. Last month. В прошлом месяце.
f PRAWSH-lum MYEH-syah-tseh.

667. Last night. Вчера вечером.
fcheh-RAH VYEH-cheh-rum.

668. Night. Ночь. *nawch.*

669. Tonight. Сегодня вечером.
syeh-VAW-dnyah VYEH-cheh-rum.

670. Yesterday. Вчера. *fcheh-RAH.*

671. Today. Сегодня. *syeh-VAW-dnyah.*

672. Day. День. *dyen^y^.*

*The twenty-four-hour system is more commonly used in Europe than in the United States. One to twelve P.M. are therefore expressed in numbers from thirteen to twenty-four.

673. Tomorrow. Завтра. *ZAHF-trah.*

674. Next week. На следующей неделе. *nah SLYEH-doo-yoo-shcheў nyeh-DYEH-lyeh.*

DAYS OF THE WEEK

675. Monday. Понедельник. *puh-nyeh-DYEL^y-n^{y}eek.*

676. Tuesday. Вторник. *FTAWR-n^{y}eek.*

677. Wednesday. Среда. *sryeh-DAH.*

678. Thursday. Четверг. *chet-VYEHRK.*

679. Friday. Пятница. *PYAHT-n^{y}ee-tsah.*

680. Saturday. Суббота. *soo-BAW-tah.*

681. Sunday. Воскресенье. *vuh-skryeh-SYEN^y-yeh.*

SEASONS AND WEATHER

682. Spring. Весна. *vyes-NAH.*

683. Summer. Лето. *LYEH-tuh.*

684. Autumn. Осень. *AW-syen^y.*

685. Winter. Зима. *z^{y}ee-MAH.*

686. It is warm. Тепло. *tyep-LAW.*

687. It is cold. Холодно. *KHAW-lud-nuh.*

688. It is raining.
Идёт дождь.
ee-DYAWT dawsht^y.

689. It is snowing.
Идёт снег.
ee-DYAWT snyek.

690. The weather is good.
Погода хорошая.
pah-GAW-duh khah-RAW-shah-yah.

691. The weather is bad.
Погода плохая.
pah-GAW-duh plah-KHAH-yah.

692. The weather is sunny.
Погода солнечная.
pah-GAW-duh SAWL-nyech-nah-yah.

693. The weather is windy.
Погода ветреная.
pah-GAW-dah VYET-ryeh-nah-yah.

694. What is the weather forecast for tomorrow?
Каково предсказание погоды на завтра?
kah-kah-VAW pryet-skah-ZAH-n^{y}ee-yeh pah-GAW-dih nah ZAHF-trah?

NUMBERS*

695. One. Один (одна, одно).
ah-D^{y}EEN (*ah-DNAH, ah-DNAW*).

Two. Два (две). *dvah* (*dvyeh*).

Three. Три. *tr^{y}ee.*

Four. Четыре. *cheh-TIH-ryeh.*

Five. Пять. *pyaht^{y}.*

Six. Шесть. *shest^{y}.*

Seven. Семь. *syem^{y}.*

Eight. Восемь. *VAW-syem^{y}.*

Nine. Девять. *DYEH-vyet^{y}.*

Ten. Десять. *DYEH-syet^{y}.*

Eleven. Одиннадцать. *ah-D^{y}EE-nah-tsaht^{y}.*

Twelve. Двенадцать. *dvyeh-NAH-tsaht^{y}.*

Thirteen. Тринадцать. *tr^{y}ee-NAH-tsaht^{y}.*

Fourteen. Четырнадцать.
cheh-TIHR-nah-tsaht^{y}.

Fifteen. Пятнадцать. *pyeht-NAH-tsaht^{y}.*

Sixteen. Шестнадцать. *shest-NAH-tsaht^{y}.*

Seventeen. Семнадцать. *syem-NAH-tsaht^{y}.*

Eighteen. Восемнадцать.
vuh-syem-NAH-tsaht^{y}.

Nineteen. Девятнадцать.
dyeh-vyet-NAH-tsaht^{y}.

Twenty. Двадцать. *DVAH-tsaht^{y}.*

Twenty-one. Двадцать один (одна, одно).
DVAH-tsaht^{y} ah-D^{y}EEN (*ah-DNAH, ah-DNAW*).

Twenty-two. Двадцать два (две).
DVAH-tsaht^{y} dvah (*dvyeh*).

Thirty. Тридцать. *TR^{y}EE-tsaht^{y}.*

Forty. Сорок. *SAW-ruk.*

Fifty. Пятьдесят. *pet^{y}-dyeh-SYAHT.*

Sixty. Шестьдесят. *shest^{y}-dyeh-SYAHT.*

*All Russian numbers are declined. The forms given here (in the nominative case) are used for counting.

Seventy. Семьдесят. *SYEM*^{y}*-dyeh-syet.*

Eighty. Восемьдесят. *VAW-syem*^{y}*-dyeh-syet.*

Ninety. Девяносто. *dyeh-vyeh-NAW-stuh.*

One hundred. Сто. *staw.*

Two hundred. Двести. *DVYEH-st*^{y}*ee.*

Three hundred. Триста. *TR*^{y}*EE-stah.*

Four hundred. Четыреста. *cheh-TIH-ryeh-stah.*

Five hundred. Пятьсот. *pet*^{y}*-SAWT.*

Six hundred. Шестьсот. *shest*^{y}*-SAWT.*

Seven hundred. Семьсот. *syem*^{y}*-SAWT.*

Eight hundred. Восемьсот. *vuh-syem*^{y}*-SAWT.*

Nine hundred. Девятьсот. *dyeh-vyet*^{y}*-SAWT.*

One thousand. Одна тысяча. *ah-DNAH TIH-syeh-chah.*

Two thousand. Две тысячи. *dvyeh TIH-syeh-chee.*

Five thousand. Пять тысяч. *pyaht*^{y} *TIH-syahch.*

One million. Один миллион. *ah-D*^{y}*EEN m*^{y}*eel*^{y}*-YAWN.*

Two million. Два миллиона. *dvah m*^{y}*eel*^{y}*-l*^{y}*ee-AW-nah.*

Six million. Шесть миллионов. *shest*^{y} *m*^{y}*eel*^{y}*-l*^{y}*ee-AW-nuf.*

INDEX

The sentences, words and phrases in this book are numbered consecutively from 1 to 695. All entries in this book refer to these numbers. In addition, each major section heading (CAPITALIZED) is indexed according to page number (**boldface**). Parts of speech are indicated by the following italic abbreviations: *adj.* for adjective, *adv.* for adverb, *n.* for noun and *v.* for verb. Parentheses are used for explanations.

Because of the large volume of material indexed, cross-indexing has generally been avoided. Phrases or groups of words will usually be found under only one of their components, e.g., "bathing suit" appears only under "bathing," even though there is a separate entry for "suit" alone. If you do not find a phrase under one word, try another.

Accept 500
across 163
address 102; mailing 41
adjust 244
afternoon, in the 663
again 29
ahead, straight 168
airline office 134
airmail 439
AIRPLANE **p. 15**
airport 199
all 126, 127; — right 24
almost 656
along 161
American 40, 113, 628; — Express 296
AMUSEMENTS **p. 40**
and 28
another (different) 518; let's have — 316
appetite, hearty 355
apple 416
architecture 460
arrive 138
ask 110
asparagus 400
aspirin 604
at 138
aunt 28
AUTOMOBILE TRAVEL **p. 19**
autumn 684

Back *adv.* 167
bad 691
bag (luggage) 124
BAGGAGE **p. 9**
baggage 118
bakery 568
balcony 483
ballet 476
bank 499
BANK AND MONEY **p. 43**
BAR, AT THE **p. 28**
barber shop 618
BARBER SHOP AND BEAUTY SALON **p. 53**
bath 262; — mat 285
bathing: — cap 528; — suit 529
battery 243
beach 489
bean 401
beauty salon 619
bed: double — 260; in — 646; twin — 261
beef 385; roast — 386
beer 313
begin 480
behind 172
belt 614
beside 171
better 512, 644
between 199
BEVERAGES **p. 35**
beyond 164
bill (banknote) 504; (= check) 294, 351, 526
birthday 34
black 556
blanket 280
blue 557; dark — 558
board, go on 188
BOAT **p. 15**
boiled 340, 411
Bolshoi Theater 477
bon voyage 189
book *n.* 582

bookstore 579
BOOKSTORE AND STATIONER'S **p. 49**
bother 81
bottle 315
boulevard 161
box 484; — office 478
boy 83
brake 244
brassiere 530
bread 358
breakfast 277, 319
BREAKFAST FOODS **p. 32**
bridge 163
bring 281
broken 109
brother 20
brown 559
building 172
bus: — service 199; — stop 215
BUS, STREETCAR AND SUBWAY **p. 17**
business 48
businessman 45
busy 54
butter 360
button 615
buy 528
by 326

Cabbage 402
cabin 195; — steward 191
cake 431
call *n.* 301; *v.* 112; — a taxi 220; — for 200; — on 31
camera 599
CAMERA STORE **p. 51**
can *v.* 87, 100
candy and pastry store 569
captain 193
car 228, 242
careful 99
carefully 116, 527; more — 225
carrot 403
cathedral 464
Catholic 452
cauliflower 404
cereal 374
chambermaid 274
change *n.* (= coins) 506; (= the rest) 453; *v.* (= convert money) 498; (= exchange) 348; (= transfer) 217
charge *n.*: admission — 481; service — 295; *v.* 203, 222; (battery) 243
cheaper 513
check *n.*: personal — 500; traveler's — 501; *v.* (baggage) 114; (= examine) 240, 245
cheese 435
cherry 417
chest 639
chicken 387; — soup 383
chocolate 436
Christmas 36
CHURCH **p. 39**
church 452–454
cigar 594
cigarette 595
CIGAR STORE **p. 51**
cigar store 593
circus 474
citizen 40
city 143
class 183–185
clean *v.* 613
clerk (female) 605; (male) 606
close *v.* 208; when does it — 467
CLOTHING **p. 46**
clothing 128; — store 570
coat 553; — hanger 288
coffee 425
cold: I am — 51; it is — 687; *n.* 632
COLORS **p. 48**
come 29; — back 279; — here 93; — in 94
comrade 8
concert 470
conductor 219
confirm 198
congratulations 33
connect 302
constipation 636
consulate 113
continue 647
CONVERSATION AT THE POST OFFICE **p. 37**
CONVERSATION ON THE TELEPHONE **p. 25**
cookie 434
corner 165
cost *v.* 510
cough *n.* 633
cream 426
credit card 230
cucumber 405
cup 425
CUSTOMS **p. 9**
customs office 117

Dance *n.* 488; *v.* 487
darker 555
daughter 17
day 672; good — 1; pe[illegible] — 459
DAYS OF THE WEEK **p. 58**
deck 196
DENTIST **p. 56**
dentist 648
department store 571
DESSERTS **p. 36**
develop 600
diarrhea 637
dictionary 584
DIFFICULTIES AND REPAIRS **p. 8**
diner (= dining car) 20[illegible]
dinner 322
direct *adj.* 139
direction 156
disturb 276
do 30, 108
dock 194
doctor 628, 629
dollar 502, 503
door 208
down 173
dress 532
drive 224
driver's license 229
drop 441
dry-cleaning service 61[illegible]
duck 388
duty (customs) 130

Early 654
east 148
egg 379–382
eight 695
eighteen 695
eighty 695
elevator 271
eleven 695
else 306
embankment 162
engine 247
engineer 44

English (language) 56
English-speaking 449
enough 346
entrance 169, 468
ENTRÉES **p. 33**
envelope 588
evening: good — 3; in the — 664
excellent 354
exchange rate 502
excuse me 74
exit 469
export 527
eye 640
eyeglasses 109

Facial *n.* 626
family 25
fat (rich food) 338
father 16
feel 642, 643
fever 634
few, a 115
fifteen 695
fifty 695
fill (prescription) 607
filling (dental) 650
film 599; color — 600
find 102
finish 133
first 183
fish *n.* 389
five 695
fix 651
flight 201
food 354
FOOD LIST **p. 31**
for 126, 181
forecast 694
foreign 498
forget 104
fork 330
form 443
forty 695
forward 296
four 695
fourteen 695
fragile 446
free (= available) 221
Friday 679
fried 339
friend 46, 101
from 206
fruit juice 371
FRUITS **p. 35**
furnished 253

Galoshes 533
garlic 366
gas station 231
GENERAL EXPRESSIONS **p. 6**
get off 219
gift 129
girl, young 84
give 239
glass 312, 427
gloves 534
go 137, 156, 157, 214, 470, 493; let's — 489
good 79, 233, 318, 648
goodbye 6
goose 390
grape 418
gravy 369
gray 560
green 561
grocery store 572
guide 457
guidebook 583

Hair 624
haircut 620
hairdresser 617
half past 657
hand 87
handbag 535
handle *v.* 116
happy: — birthday 34; — New Year 35
hardware store 579
hat 536
have to 217
he 104
headache 630
health: — certificate 121; to your — 317
HEALTH AND ILLNESS **p. 54**
hear 485
hello (telephone) 299
here 47; — is 118
honey 377
horseback riding 494
hotel 102, 251
HOTEL AND APARTMENT **p. 21**
hour 115; per — 222
how 91; — are you 22; — do you do 5; — far 154; — long (time) 137; — many 202; — much 131
hundred: one — 695; two — 695
hungry, I am 53
hurt 649
husband 14

I 8
ice 356, 357; — cream 436
identification card 120
if 326
immediately 607
important 80
in 241
included 295, 350
indicate 445
indigestion 638
inexpensive 252
insure 444
interested, I am 460
intermission 486
international 229
Intourist 136
introduce 11
it 80

Jacket 537
jam 376
jewelry store 574
juice 371–373

Key 106; room — 290
kilo 202
kilometer, per 223
kind: what — of 594
knife 331
know 63, 603
kopeck 439

Ladies' room 89
Lake Ladoga 138
lamb 391
large 504
larger 514
late 655
later 522
laundry 609
LAUNDRY AND DRY CLEANING **p. 52**
lead *v.* 235
leave 206, 293
left, to the 151
lemon 419
lemonade 429
length 520
less 345
letter 291
letters abroad 441
lettuce 406

licensed 457
lighter *adj.* (color) 554; *n.* 596
listen 98
liter 239
little, a 59
liver 392
lobster 393
long distance 297
look for 101
lose 103, 650
lost-and-found bureau 110
lubricate 242
lunch (= midday meal) 320

Magazine 585
mail 296
mailbox 441
make 521; — out 294
MAKING YOURSELF UNDERSTOOD **p. 5**
man 85
manager 289
manicure 627
map 238, 587
marketplace 575
match *n.* 598
matinée 471
may I 31, 182
mayonnaise 368
me 62, 100
meal 264
mean *v.* 67
measurements 519
meat 341; — market 576
mechanic 232
medium (meat) 342
melon 420
mend 611
men's room 88
menu 327
message 305
middle, in the 166
militiaman 112
militia station 111
milk 427
million, one 695
mine 124
minister 450
minute 298, 301
miss *v.* 248
mistake 351
moment 95
Monday 675
money 104, 498
month 666
more 344
morning: good — 2; in the — 662
mother 15
motor 248
movies 472
Mr. 9
Mrs. 10
much: how — 131; very — 75
mug 313
museum 465
mushroom 407
must 130
mustard 367
my 13, 14, 38

Name: my — is 38; what is your — 37
napkin 329
nausea 635
nearest 593
necessary 127
necktie 551
new 616
newspaper 586
newsstand 581
New Year 35
New York 41
next 674
night 668; good — 4; last — 667
nightgown 539
nine 695
nineteen 695
ninety 695
no 71
north 146
not 336
nothing 125
now, not 97
NUMBERS **p. 59**
nylon 548

Oatmeal 375
obliged 175
o'clock 656
office 134
oil (food) 364; (lubricating) 240
old, years 39
omelet 378
on 159
one 695
onion 408
open *v.* 127, 207; when does it — 466
opera 475
opposite 170
orange (color) 562; (fruit) 421
orchestra (section) 482
order *v.* 335, 347
other 160
overheat 247
oysters 394

Pack *n.* 595
package 115
pain 639
painting 461
pair 541
paper: toilet — 283; writing — 592
park *n.* 170; — of Culture and Rest 214; *v.* 250
pass 358
passport 119
pay *v.* 130, 131
pea 409
peach 422
pen, fountain 591
pencil 590
pepper (seasoning) 363; (vegetable) 410
per 222
perhaps 72
permanent *n.* 625
permit me 11
personal 126, 500
PERSONAL MATTERS **p. 3**
PHARMACY **p. 52**
pharmacy 603
pie 432
piece 432
pillow 281
pillowcase 282
pink 563
pipe 597
plain 335
plane 197, 198
plate 332
pleasant 27
please 73
pork 395
possible: as soon as — 294; if — 326
postcard 589
potato 411, 412
prescription 607
press *v.* 613

price 511
priest 449
Protestant 453
pull out 652
purchase *n.* 526
purple 564
purser 192
put in 616

Quarter: — past 658; — to 659

Rabbi 451
radiator 491
railroad station 204
raining, it is 688
raincoat 540
rare (meat) 341
raspberry 423
read 58
ready 601
receipt 447
recommend 318
red 565
regards, give 28
regular 439
rent 228
repair 246
repeat 65
reservation 181, 197, 254; — window 177
restaurant 318
RESTAURANT, AT THE **p. 28**
return 522
rice 413
right (= correct) 156; to the — 150
road 233
roll (bread) 359; (film) 549
room (hotel) 255; double — 257; — number 292; — service 272; single — 256
rough 234
Russian (language) 59; — Orthodox 454

Safe deposit box 259
salad 348
salesgirl 524
salesman 525
salt 362
sardine 396
Saturday 680
sauce 370
sausage 397
say 69
school 171
sculpture 462
SEASONS AND WEATHER **p. 58**
seat 181
second 184
section: business — 140; residential — 141; shopping — 142
see 8, 268, 485
send 273
serve 323
service 354; (religious) 456
set *v.* 625
seven 695
seventeen 695
seventy 695
several 266
sew 615
shade (color) 554
shave 622
she 103
sheet 284
ship *v.* 523
shirt 546, 611
shoe (ladies') 541; (men's) 542; — store 577
shoelace 543
SHOPPING **p. 44**
shopping, go 507
short 621
should 157
show *v.* 140, 238
shower 263
side 159
sight (place) 463
SIGHTSEEING **p. 39**
sister 19
sit 26
six 695
sixteen 695
sixty 695
size 518
skating 495
skiing 496
skirt 544
sleep 641
sleeper (train) 210
slipper 545
slowly, more 60
small 505
smaller 515
snack 321
snowing, it is 689
soap 286
soccer game 490
SOCIAL CONVERSATION **p. 1**
socks 547
something 335, 640
son 18
soon 294
soup 383, 384
south 147
Soviet Union 587
speak 56, 57, 59, 289, 457
spicy 336
spinach 414
SPORTS **p. 42**
spring (season) 682
stairs 173
stall *v.* 248
stamp 441
starch 612
stationer's 580
stay 305
steak 398
steward 190
stocking 548
stop *v.* 226; bus — 215
store 574; department — 571
STORES **p. 48**
strawberry 424
street 152, 159
streetcar 214
stronger 516
student 42
subway 216
sugar 361
suit 549
suitcase 127
summer 683
Sunday 681
sunny 692
supper 323
sweater 550
sweet 337
swimming 497; — pool 492
synagogue 455

Table 326
tablespoon 334
tailor 578
take 202
TAXI **p. 18**
taxi 220
tea 428; — cozy 446
teacher 43
teaspoon 333

telephone number 300
tell 100, 219
temporarily 651
ten 695
thanks 75
that 158
there (thither) 155; from — 485; over — 124
these 129, 130
thing 130; same — 518
think so 64
third 185
thirsty, I am 52
thirteen 695
thirty 695
this 12, 116, 157, 159
thousand 695
three 695
throat 631
Thursday 678
ticket: one-way — 179; — reservation office 135; reserved-seat — 180; round-trip — 178; — window 176
TICKETS **p. 14**
TIME **p. 56**
time 521; at what — 200; on — 201; until next — 7; what — is it 653
tip *n.* 350
tire *n.* 245; flat — 246
tired, I am 55
to 137, 139, 146
toast 376
tobacco 597
today 671
tomato 415
tomorrow 673
tonight 669
too (overly) 336
tooth 649
towel 287
town 236; out of — 145
track 206
traffic light 164
TRAIN **p. 16**
train 205; express — 187; local — 186
transfer *n.* 218
transit, in 123
TRAVEL DIRECTIONS **p. 11**
traveling 49
trip 647
trouble, no 308
trousers 552
try on 517
Tuesday 676
turn 146
twelve 695
twenty 695
twenty-one 695
twenty-two 695
two 695

Uncle 28
understand 61, 62
underwear 538
United States 438
university 216
until 276
upstairs 269
us 29
use *n.* 126

Vacation 47
vanilla 437
veal 399
vegetable: — oil 364; — soup 384
VEGETABLES AND SALADS **p. 34**
very 23
village 144
vinegar 365
visa, visitor's 122
vodka 311

Wait 95, 608
waiter 324
waitress 325
wake 275
walk 155
wallet 105
want 8
warm: I am — 50; it is — 686
wash 87, 611, 618
water 241; mineral — 315; soda — 430
way 139, 140; on the — 182; that — 158; this — 157
we 457
weather 690; — forecast 694
Wednesday 677
week 674
welcome, you are 76
well *adj.* 23; — done (meat) 343
west 149
what 37, 152; — are you doing 30; — do you wish 92; — is this 68
when 138
where 87
while, a 250
white 566
who 82; — is it 278
why 90
width 520
wife 13
window 207, 326
windy 693
wine 314; — list 328
winter 685
wish 92, 508
with 356
without 264, 357
woman 86
woolen 550
word 67
work (= function) 249
worse 645
wrap 527
write 66

Year 665
yellow 567
yes 70
yesterday 670
yet 96
you 11, 23; to — 175
your 28, 37

Zipper 616